Praise for *The Money Chimp*

"If your intention is to build wealth and be financially free then your journey starts by investing in your own personal development and improving your financial literacy. *The Money Chimp* is a must-read for anyone who needs to learn how to manage their money especially 18-25s."

Steve Bolton
CEO, *Platinum Property Partners*

"If you require an easy to understand book that highlights all the key areas to help you make and retain money, then buy this book."

Nicholas Charles FCCA
The Charles Group UK

"This is the best book on managing money for 18-25s I have read. If you are 18-25 (or older) and you follow the steps in this book, you will be free of money worries for the rest of your life!"

Karen Sutton-Johal
Debt Advisor, *The 4 Money Mindsets*

"A must-read for anyone who wants to understand their relationship with money. Loads of recommendations and smart tips with lots of relevant examples and anecdotes. We all should take actionable steps by doing a comprehensive fact-find then creating a *Lifestyle Financial Plan*. After-all, life is not a rehearsal! And take *The Money Chimp* test."

Simon Jeffries
Founder/MD, *Asset Wealth Creation*

"A wonderful book from the master of business coaches, Andrew Priestley. While it is not always possible to put wise heads on young shoulders, this book goes a long way towards achieving that. Financial literacy should be a central part of our education system and this book provides the knowledge and the strategy for all young people to develop financial street smarts."

Andrew Fuller
Clinical Psychologist/Family Therapist
Bestselling Author, Resilient Youth Australia

"This is a must-read for those who are serious about building wealth. You won't learn this information at school which is why 18-25s are the most susceptible to chronic debt. Filled with practical case studies, money management techniques and wealth generation ideas this book is a great tool for debt busting and helping you create the wealth you need to live your best life on purpose."

Sonia Brown MBE
Founder/Director, *National Black Women's Network*

"We educate our children in maths and while there is growing awareness of the need to educate them in money management this is happening too slowly and doesn't help those who have already left school or a building up university debt. This book is a quick way to become financially skilled with practical solutions all presented in an easy read. It's targeted at young adults but I think it gives such good practical advice that you can put into action and benefit from whatever age you are."

Sonia Gill
Educator, Author, Founder/Director, *Heads Up (UK)*

"Andrew Priestley says that people tend to write some *software* in their heads about money when they are kids and don't update the *files* later in life. I believe him. The useful and practical tips in this well-researched and readable book may be just what the doctor ordered to update your files and re-order your mindset, beliefs and perceptions about money. Written in a relaxed, park-bench chat style, *The Money Chimp* makes the complex simple, and shows that you don't have to be a reader of the *Financial Times* to learn to implement the habits and skills of good money management. Reading it will be one of the best decisions you ever make."

Charles Hammond
Pastor, *Elim Pentecostal Church, West London*

"So many young people turn to credit cards to temporarily achieve a sense of freedom. Learn Andrew's five skills and five habits and you will achieve a life free from debt and anxiety. This is a must-read for every young person and every adult struggling to get out from under their debt."

Shirley McKinnon
Author of *Coach Yourself to Wealth*

"*The Money Chimp* is an insightful and actionable guidebook that will not only inspire you but also instruct you on how to make and manage your money. This is essential reading for anyone looking for clearly defined strategies on how to financially move forward and create a clear game plan. As a mother of six and grandmother of five, *The Money Chimp* hits the mark."

Sharon Tan
Living with Purpose Coach and Speaker

"I have been an adviser 26 years and read more books on this subject than I care to recall. Most are dry and academic and over-complicated. *The Money Chimp* however manages to address money issues in a logical fashion with an easy to follow structure. This little book addresses the core of money management and offers readers realistic and practical solutions. I have no doubt it will have a huge impact on people's lives."

Susan Bryant, Principal/Financial Adviser
Seeds of Advice, Financial Planning for Rural Families

What people are saying about *The Money Chimp* test

"*The Money Chimp* test is bang on target. Brilliant."
Ken, Financial Advisor

"It was frighteningly accurate and gave me the big wake-up call I needed to sort out my finances."
Steven, Software designer

"The report described my money managing skills to a tee and highlighted the blind spots with practical recommendations."
Errol, Life Skills trainer

"Amazing! Annoyingly grabbed the total attention of my 19 and 25 year olds."
Mark, Father of two young adults

Take the *Money Chimp* online test at

https://www.moneychimp.net

Search *Multiply Your Money* on *Facebook, YouTube* and *Spotify*

The Money Chimp

Spend less, save more, and get out of debt faster

Andrew Priestley

WRITINGMATTERS

The Money Chimp Updated

First published in January 2016
Second reprint January 2020

Writing Matters Publishing

ISBN 978-1-7118087-7-2 (pbk)

ISBN 978-0-9575440-8-6 (ebook)

The rights of Andrew Priestley to be identified as the author of this work have been asserted in accordance with Sections 77 and 78 of the Copyright Designs and Patents Act, 1988.

A CIP catalogue record for this book is available from the British Library.

All rights reserved. No part of this book may be reproduced in material (including photocopying or storing in any medium by electronic means and whether or not transiently or incidentally to some other use of this publication) without the written permission of the copyright holder except in accordance with the provisions of the Copyright, design and Patents Act 1988. Applications for the Copyright holders written permission to reproduce any part of this publication should be addressed to the publisher.

Copyright 2015-2020 Andrew Priestley

Please Note: This book, *The Money Chimp Updated* and *The Money Chimp* quiz are intended as information only and do not constitute specific financial, investment, taxation or legal advice unique to your situation. It is for educational purposes only. Its sole aim is to help you become better at understanding managing your own money. The Author, Publisher and Resellers accept no responsibility for loss, damage or injury to persons or their belongings as a direct or indirect result of reading this book.

Contents

1	Testimonials
11	***The Money Chimp* At A Glance**
15	**Part 1: Before We Get Started**
17	Monkey Magic
19	Are You A Champ With Money?
21	The End Of The Tunnel
23	The Truth About Most 18-25 Year Olds And Money
25	A Picture Is Worth A Thousand Words
29	The Three Top Money Managing Tips
31	**Money Tip #1 Spend Less Than You Earn**
33	**Money Tip #2 Plan For The Future**
35	Back To The Future ... Again
39	Cradle To Grave
43	Time To Put The Book Down For A Minute
45	These Predictions Are Not Fixed In Concrete
49	**Money Tip #3 Make Your Money, Make *More* Money**
53	Two Big Show Stoppers
59	What Is Money?
61	OK, I'm Stuck

63	So, Let's Talk About Credit Cards
67	Listen To Your Money Talk
69	**Part 2 The Five Habits And Five Skills**
71	Is Managing Your Money A Science Or An Art?
75	Your Performance Plan
77	What Is Money …Again?
79	Take *The Money Chimp* Quiz
81	The Top 10 Money Managing Principles
83	Time To Review
85	**Part 3 The Five Money Activities**
87	**Money Activity #1 Earning**
89	Three Sources Of Income
91	Earn More Than 'Just Enough'
99	**Money Activity #2 Spending**
103	Get Receipts For Everything And Read Your Bank Statements
111	**Money Activity # 3 Saving**
117	Warning: You Are Not An ATM Or An Interest-Free Bank
119	Get The Facts First
121	**Money Activity #4 Investing**
127	**Money Activity #5 Giving**
129	What About Giving To Family And Friends?
135	**Part 4 The Five Money Managing Skills**
137	**Money Skill #1 Monitoring**

143	**Money Skill #2 Focusing**
151	**Money Skill #3 Reducing Your Spending**
157	**Money Skill #4 Developing Your Financial Smarts**
161	Take The Money Managing Skills Quiz
165	**Money Skill #5 Taking Action**
171	The Bonus Principle
173	**Part 5 What To Do If You Are In Debt**
175	Do You Have A Debt Problem?
181	If You Need To Be Debt-Free
187	Will You Learn To Manage Your Money And Stay Out Of Debt?
189	A Final Word On Credit Cards
191	Oh Yes … Black Friday, Cyber Monday, Christmas, Boxing Day, January Sales …
193	Let Me Know How You Are Going
195	**References**
197	About Andrew Priestley
199	Contacts And Links

THE MONEY CHIMP

The Money Chimp at a glance and why you should read it

Extensive review

The Money Chimp is the result of an extensive review of money management books, websites and courses. The purpose of *The Money Chimp* is help readers spend less, save more and get out of debt faster - especially credit card debt.

10 Money Managing Habits and Skills

The review identified five key areas for managing money - *(earning, spending, saving, investing, giving)*; and five practical money management skills - *(monitoring, focusing, reducing, training* and *taking action)*.

Most young professionals focus on *earning* and *spending* but neglect the other eight skills.

While many books include some of these key areas the author believes this is the first time all ten key areas have been covered in one book.

18-25s (and older) can be debt-free in 90 days

The book is geared towards young professionals - 18-25s - because typically they spend 130% of their weekly income; and are the most likely to enter a cycle of chronic debt.

But it is suited for anyone who needs to manage their money more effectively. Most readers, for example will experience the benefits of the strategies and steps and can even become debt-free within 90 days.

You might be single or in a relationship. If you are single the challenge is take charge of your finances while you are independent and answerable only to yourself. If you are in a relationship, it's important to openly discuss financial issues with your partner and master these skills together.

Road-tested live in workshops

All material, activities and practical suggestions were road-tested in one-day workshops and three-month courses. No matter how interesting, if an idea didn't work in a live workshop, *it's not in this book*.

Pounds and dollars

The author works in the UK, Australia and the USA and the examples are a mixture of pounds and dollars.

Take the online test

You can rate your strengths in the 10 money managing principles by taking *The Money Chimp test* at:

www.moneychimp.net

Get a comprehensive report

The Money Chimp test generate a comprehensive 20-page money-managing report with practical recommendations and options.

Personalised feedback

The report is helpful because you get personalised feedback to every question you answer.

Join the *Facebook* group *Multiply Your Money*

You can join the *Multiply Your Money* group on *Facebook* that contains, videos, handouts and other resources as a well as a growing community sharing their experiences of *The Money Chimp*.

Search *Multiply Your Money*

Multiply Your Money is available on *YouTube, Facebook, LinkedIn, Apple Podcasts* and *Spotif.*

Award winning, #1 ranked author

Andrew Priestley is an award-winning, qualified business coach ranked within the top 100 Entrepreneur Mentors UK, best-selling author and speaker.

The goal of *The Money Chimp* is to help young professionals understand and master personal finance.

Part 1

Before We Get Started

Monkey Magic

I remember one Christmas I got a fantastic game called *Barrel of Monkeys* from Santa that is as popular now as it was then.

You get a little barrel containing 12 plastic monkeys with big curly arms. You start the game by shaking up the barrel and tipping out the monkeys. Then you pick up one monkey and use that monkey's arms to pick up another monkey. Then you use that second monkey to link to a third and so on.

You get a point for every monkey picked up but if you drop a monkey it's the next player's turn. The winner is the player with the most points.

The winner is a *champ* and the losers are *chumps*!

It's exciting fun but it's a game of skill and harder than it sounds. You have to proceed carefully. And to win you have to think about what you are doing.

My personal best was six monkeys but the world speed record holder - a 50 year old doctor - linked all 12 monkeys in about two minutes.

Managing your money is a lot like *Barrel of Monkeys:* a game of skill that takes practice.

The rules aren't difficult but likewise you have to keep playing and think about what you are doing. You might need to proceed slowly and be willing to learn from mistakes. And like any board game, such as *Monopoly, Cashflow 101,* or digital console games, the more you play the better you get.

Winning is a challenge but as your *skills and capabilities* develop you start winning and having more fun. And the more little wins you achieve the more you *believe* you can win.

Losing is very predictable. If you rush and don't think about what you're doing you will lose.

Managing your money is just as fun as any kids game but the stakes are a lot higher.

Like a game, you can learn from experience and your mistakes but the fastest way to start winning is to learn the rules. The good news is managing your money has some basic rules that are easy to learn.

Once you start playing by the rules the sooner you start winning the money managing game, and life gets better.

Want to know the rules? Then keep reading!

Are You A Champ With Money?

Get a pen and underline any of the questions below that sound like you.

- *Are you careless with spending?*
- *Are you poor at managing money?*
- *Do you earn enough?*
- *Do you have problems budgeting?*
- *Are you hopeless at saving?*
- *Do you feel there's never enough?*
- *Do you watch TV shows of the rich and famous then feel envious or cynical about people who earn big bucks?*
- *Do you feel unlucky?*
- *Do you feel annoyed when ordinary people win millions on the lottery?*
- *Do you think it's unfair that you didn't?*

- *Do you wonder where all your money goes?*
- *Does money slip through your fingers like sand?*
- *Do you run out of money before the next payday?*
- *Does it usually feel like there is more month than money?*
- *Do you waste money on stuff you don't really need?*
- *Do you borrow money from family or friends?*
- *Do you spend too much on credit at Christmas?*
- *Do you often 'max out' your credit card?*
- *Are you usually late paying bills?*
- *Do you usually incur late fees?*

If you answered YES to just one of these questions – and I really do mean *just one* – then this book is for you.

You will discover ten time-tested principles for managing money that can even have you debt-free within 90 days if you really apply what you learn.

The Money Chimp is especially relevant for 18-25 year olds because they are the most likely to waste money and enter a cycle of chronic debt. But this is really useful information for *anyone* who knows they need to manage their money better.

But lets focus on young adults for a moment. Why are they so prone to debt?

The End Of The Tunnel

In 2009, we experienced a global financial crisis (GFC) that started to lift in 2016. But the truth is young people in *any* economy suffer from money worries, are under immense pressure to part with their cash *and more likely to go into debt*.

According to the charity *Mybnk*, 90% of Brits have no financial education. Brits currently owe £72.5bn on credit cards and youth credit card debt is a staggering £9.7bn. That's why *Mybnk* specialises in educating young people aged 7-25 on the skills and capabilities they need to learn in order to manage their money ... for life.

UK wealth coach, Simon Jeffries says, "Younger adults do not like to think about money until they are in their late 20s. They want to party! They live by the acronym *FOMO - Fear Of Missing Out* - even if that puts them into debt."

The problem is 18-25s are now the most likely to enter a chronic cycle of crippling lifetime debt unless they change their skills, behaviours and attitudes around money.

I was motivated to write this book because I know bright, aspiring young people in this age group. And I do not want them to ever stress and struggle over money, now or later in life.

Over several years, I read books, hundreds of online articles and attended over 40 courses on managing money. And identified ten money principles that we all need to understand.

You might already know some of the principles in this book - *and resisting them*. And I am sure some will be brand new to you.

But I believe that this is the first time these ten proven money-managing principles have all appeared in the *one* book and in this unique format.

Importantly, you will discover ten time-tested principles designed to get you debt-free in the next 90 days.

If you are in the 18-25 age zone then this book aims to inspire you to spend less, save more and get out of debt faster - especially credit card debt. (In fact, most young people can be debt free within 90 days.)

These principles will save you time, money and stress. And it might make you debt-free, financially free and wealthier.

But the principles in this book aren't just for young adults. They apply to *anyone* of *any age* with limiting beliefs, poor values and attitudes, bad habits or undeveloped skills around money.

In addition to the book, you can take *The Money Chimp* test online to see *exactly* how you rate *right now* in these ten principles. *The Money Chimp* test takes about seven minutes to complete online and you immediately get back a comprehensive, personalised PDF money managing report.

Take the test right now at:

www.moneychimp.net

And please search *Multiply Your Money* on *Facebook* and *LinkedIn* and join the group for free videos and downloads; *YouTube* for videos and and *Spotify* for the podcast series.

The Truth About Most 18-25 Year Olds And Money

Did you know most 18-25 year olds spend 130% of their weekly *disposable income?* If you earn a £100 a week this means you spend £130, on average. But how is that even possible?

Basically, they spend the extra money on credit cards. Young people in the UK owe a staggering £9.7bn with the average young person being £2886.48 in the red.

Well, you will spend money on food shopping, rent, utilities and transport, right? But then there's your *discretionary income* - money available to save, invest or spend after you've paid your bills, necessities and taxes. What do you spend *that* money on?

Typically, most of your discretionary money is spent on things you don't really need and can't afford. And your spending is powered by an ingrained *buy now/pay later* mentality.

Typically, you are about two pay days - four if you are lucky - from being flat broke. If you usually live beyond your means you'll have this fantasy of getting a better job, a pay rise, winning the lottery or receiving a windfall (inheritance).

The truth is most young people get into the habit of being bailed out by some benevolent person (usually their mum or dad, relatives or friends). Or if you are like most young adults you get into the habit of racking up debt on a credit card.

Sadly, most young people have never been taught how to do the most important life skill ever – managing your money. And so pretty soon, you are spending more than you earn, *plus* racking up credit card debt *plus* the interest, fees and charges that go with abusing bank credit.

This describes most older people too.

A recent survey showed 89% of wage earners - *of any age group* - can't maintain their lifestyle beyond six weeks if they lose their job. If this sounds very much like you - then unless you change - you will experience the effect of poor money habits, too.

The good news is you can change! The principles in this book are easy to learn, they work and they will work for you.

For now, understand this: There are two main types of money managers: *spenders* and *investors*. The average person is a *spender*. Basically, spenders *spend more than they earn*. Investors *spend less than they earn* ... and invest. It's that simple.

And investors are more mature and responsible with money; whereas spenders are more immature and irresponsible with money.

Which one accurately describes you right now?

Look, before we go any further I want to give you an interesting little exercise that involves some web searching.

A Picture Really Is Worth A Thousand Words

I have studied the personal finances of people living in three Western economies – the UK, USA and Australia. So, let's start with those three countries. I want you to fire up your web browser and type in UK, USA or Australian *spending habits infographic*.

I've selected these three countries because their governments publish reasonably accurate and up-to-date financial data related to average household income and expenditure.

An infographic displays complex information as a picture rather than wads of text and data. I like infographics because you can quickly see what's happening rather than having to wade through a written report.

I found an infographic produced by the *Australian Securities and Investment Commission* (ASIC) very interesting. It clearly illustrated how most *ordinary* householders spend their household income.

In that year, the total annual household income was AUD$642 billion. *What* they spent their money on was fascinating. For example, Australians spent $2.7 billion on vegetables, $5.4 billion on chocolate ... and $9.5 billion on dental!

They spent $10 billion on beauty treatments , $9 billion on games and gadgets, $5 billion on fashion, $2.68 billion going to the cinema ... but only $2 billion on education and $0.78 billion on self-improvement.

We can infer Australians need to make some better spending choices.

The UK infographic is equally fascinating. It shows Brits earn on average £29.4K per annum and their highest expenses are housing, transport and food.

I was interested in how Brits spend their discretionary income (money left over after paying household bills). Music is a high priority in Northern Ireland, sport is the highest discretionary expenditure in the north of England and Londoners spend the most on spas and beauty treatments!

There is a revealing infographic that shows that 18-25s are the most susceptible to debt; 35-45s have the least amount of discretionary spend; and 54-65s are the best savers.

The USA householder stats show very similar patterns.

So, the activity is to get *Googling*. Make sure you click on the *Images* tab and include the word *infographic* in your search.

Start with Australia, UK and USA because I know you will find some useful infographics. By the way, I looked at infographics over the past five years and it seems spending patterns have not changed much.

If you don't live in these three countries, then *Google your country* and see what you can find. I'll wait.

OK, you're back. So what did you discover and what does all this mean to you?

Well firstly, it should give you an indication of how much people in your country currently earn and what they spend their money on annually. And therefore because you live in that country what *you* might also expect to earn and spend.

Obviously, there are exceptions to the national averages but for now all we need is a thought-provoking snapshot and a heads-up.

The average UK income is currently £29.4k (2019). Tax aside, if you spent 130% of that income you would have spent £38,220 - an additional £8,820! And that extra £8,820 is debt.

And of concern, studies say this is the norm.

The Money Chimp gets you to explore two important questions. Firstly, *Do you know what you spend your money on?* (You need to know.)

And: *Is there a possibility that you can actually spend less than you earn?* (So that you are spending less and saving more.)

And the answer should be *Yes* to both.

I want to emphasise that there is so much useful information on the web about managing your money, personal finance, budgeting, saving money, reducing debt and so on. And I was surprised by the amount of first-rate, free, online personal finance courses, too.

All you need to do is search. But start by looking online at infographics.

I think I am already capable and skilled at managing my personal finances but even I got some useful tips on how to improve things just by looking at the householder data from several countries.

Starting with eating less chocolate!

The Three Top Money-Managing Tips

Money works along fixed principles of cause and effect and the principles are straightforward and easy to understand. The right way to manage your money is time-tested, proven and established. We know what works and what doesn't.

We know that *spender*s spend more than they earn and *investors* spend less than they earn, save up and invest.

I did a search on the top money managing tips of all time. They are:

1. Spend less that you earn
2. Plan for the future; and
3. Make your money make *more* money.

Let's look at each principle in more detail.

Money Tip #1
Spend Less Than You Earn

The most sensible money management tip has to be:

Spend less than you earn.

In Charles Dickens' classic novel *David Copperfield*, the character Wilkins Micawber gives the much quoted recipe for happiness:

> Annual income twenty pounds, annual expenditure
> nineteen, nineteen and six, result happiness.
> Annual income twenty pounds, annual expenditure
> twenty pounds ought and six, result misery.

In plain English - no matter what century you live in - if you earn £20 and spend *less* than £20 you are OK. If you earn £20 and spend *more* than £20, you are in trouble!

In these days of easy credit, I would amend this advice to:

*Don't spend more money
than you can afford to repay.*

When *David Copperfield* was written in 1850, the general public did not have access to banking, lending and personal finance tools such as credit cards and personal loans.

And there was no welfare system. Abject poverty *was* truly bleak, soul destroying and abject, and as Dickens described.

People who went into debt often ended up in a lifetime of the lowliest and meagre servitude.

There is a difference between *good* and *bad* debt. Taking a mortgage on a family home is *good debt* (or any borrowings that are tax deductible), whereas borrowing money to buy expensive wearable technology or a new car qualifies as *bad debt*.

A mortgage is considered *good debt* because a house is an investment that *can* go up in value and yield profit when sold in the future (but not always); while borrowing to purchase consumer items is considered *bad debt* because these items usually decrease in resale value. Immediately.

There is a lot to be said for living within your current means. This does not mean you should accept your current level of income. Aim to improve your current income, but at any level aim to live below that level.

In fact, aim to create a *surplus of cash*.

Money Tip #2
Plan For The Future

It makes sense to plan for future financial needs. But I understand that when you are 18 it is hard enough imagining being 25 or 30 let alone trying to imagine a time when you will be in your 60s or 70s retired and living on a pension (if pensions will even exist in your future). Subsequently, most young people can't be bothered planning a month ahead, let alone a year.

Most young people say, "I'll make the money first *and then I'll plan for the future."* But every money expert says the time to plan for the future is now or as early as possible.

I recently heard of a bright, young, hard-working software coder who started his own business. His income has grown from £24k to £84k a year and he has bought a small apartment. Wisely, he has invested in ISAs and a pension scheme and is on target to being financially independent ... by his early 40s.

He may be an exception to the rule but the point is: *when would now be a good time to think about your future?*

Just remember: *spenders* spend more than they earn; *investors* spend less, save ... and invest.

THE MONEY CHIMP

Back To The Future ... Again

The future is a lot more predictable than you think (flying cars, self-lacing trainers and hover boards aside.)

Most governments have something like a *national bureau of statistics* that identifies both short and long-range trends. They carefully analyse these trends to plan ahead.

There is a phenomenon called the *Baby Bocmers,* the generation born between the years 1946 and 1964. After the Second World War (1945) there was a massive spike in the population unlike anything seen before.

Imagine a python swallowed a pig whole. You would see this huge bump as that pig slowly passes through the digestive tract of the python.

Well, that's how economist David Cork imagined the *Baby Boomer* phenomenon. The *pig* is the *Baby Boomers* and the python is a *time* line. Cork's book, *The Pig and The Python,* explores the economic trends associated with *Baby Boomers* as they age and move through time.

He suggests that the most profitable trends have always been associated with the current age of the boomers.

So when the *Boomers* were infants, baby wear boomed. When the *Boomers* went to school, education boomed. When the *Boomers* became teenagers, teen fashion and music boomed. As adults, the *Boomers* needed housing and food, so, housing and supermarkets boomed. Therefore, any stocks and shares associated *with those trends* also boomed.

The first of the *Boomers* started to turn 70 in 2016. The big money making trends will include things such as aged care, medtech, biotech, nutrition, tourism, retirement communities and finance to name some of the industries that will grow.

Governments are looking *very* closely at these trends.

As more *Boomers* exit the workforce, there will be less taxpayers. That places a massive financial drain on most governments. That's why they are extending the retirement age, reducing welfare, eliminating pensions and aged benefits and introducing new laws and tax incentives in workplaces, and encouraging self-funded pension schemes.

The question at any age is: *Do I have enough money?* More so, if you are thinking ahead to retiring.

In Lee Eisenberg's book, *The Number,* he asks, *What do you need financially for the rest of your life and what will it cost to retire?* This book is not for the faint-hearted. If you think that one day you will retire with a pension, and, have enough to live on, think again.

Most likely you will need to self-fund your retirement and lifestyle because most Western governments are going to phase out pensions and state benefits.

Even the key message of a much softer guide to planning for the future *Planning for Retirement* by Patrick Grant can be summed up by saying *the sooner you start* saving money in a pension scheme the more money you will have when you retire. In other words: *Start now!*

The good news is: even a little consistently saved and invested *now* will grow into a significant lump sum ... later.

So, start sooner.

National Bureaus of Statistics can suggest how your life will run from cradle to the grave because they have the research data and have analysed the trends in order to plan for the future needs of the population.

A great example of forward planning is the vast amount of money London is spending, now, on developing the new inner city cross rail links and nationwide high speed train networks, now, in anticipation of growing needs 25 years ... from now.

The *London Underground* is upgrading a 50 year old signaling system to meet demands ... 50 years from now.

However, governments now want you to do your bit in planning your financial future. Now.

In fact, you may not have a choice.

THE MONEY CHIMP

Cradle To Grave

So, here are the stages of life flagged by statisticians that will cost you money; and require you to plan ahead.

Childhood and teens - education

In Western countries, you will go into child care, then kindergarten and then primary school. Then you will go to secondary school. You will need bassinets and prams and bikes and uniforms and dental and sports equipment and toys … and stuff … and more stuff that kids need and want.

At about 17, you will either go on to do tertiary education, adult education, get an apprenticeship, seek employment or you will start your own business. (I am assuming you do not have ambitions to become a career welfare benefits recipient.)

Adolescence to early adult

If you go down the tertiary education/apprenticeship route you will finish education or training by about age 23.

Some will complete education later, if you take a gap year or defer for a time. Many young adults are keen to travel in their early to mid 20s and do take a gap year to explore the world.

From 18, trying out adulthood, exploring relationships and getting established in work, takes priority.

Statistically, by late 20s you might still looking for the right job. Emotionally and biologically you are looking for the right partner. Some partner younger of course, but it appears this generation is finding Mr or Miss Right much later.

And they are marrying (or civil partnering) later. Marriage used to be popular in the early 20s, then mid to late 20s and now marriage is often postponed until early 30s.

Statistics show that 18-25s are the most susceptible to chronic debt. If you go to university you will most likely graduate with a student loan debt that on average takes another seven years to pay off.

By late 20s you have probably stabilised your job and partner search and you are most probably looking for a home of your own especially if you've found your mate.

Millennials (Gen X and Gen Ys born from 1982 to early 2004) is the next major population trend (also called *Echo Boomers*). This new generation is more interested in experiences and rental accommodation than home ownership.

They spend up big on fashion, gadgets and technology, socialising and travel. And that is why experts see this generation as highly susceptible to credit card debt.

Adulthood and new family (35-45s)

At this stage, statistically, you are now thinking about a home loan. If you are 35 plus and take a 25-year mortgage you are expecting to carry that loan until around age 60.

However, rarely will you stay in the same house. You may even sell that home at a profit and use the equity gained to finance your next home. We used to move homes every ten years but now it's about every seven years. On this basis, you will probably mortgage at least three to four family homes in your lifetime.

While couples are marrying later, most are still thinking about starting a family. But medically, there is added pressure to have children *before* you reach your 40s.

A priority will be stabilising your income because you need to pay for child care, kindergarten, primary and secondary school, medical, dental etc. Insurances start to make a lot more sense. (If you have a mortgage, house and life insurance will probably e a condition of the loan.)

People in the 35-45 age range have the least amount of disposable income and as stated 18-25s are the most likely to already be in a cycle of bad debt.

Even though retirement seems way off it is probably a good idea to start thinking about *saving* if not growing a pension pot.

Locate *lost* pensions

You have probably already worked in several jobs and acquired several pension schemes without even knowing you were enrolled in one. It's money most people don't even know they have; or recall having.

By the way, there is a massive fund of unclaimed pension money held by most governments. Helping people find and consolidate their *lost* pension funds is a growth industry.

You can help yourself by first compiling a list of all your past jobs. Maybe *you* already have a small sum of cash wa ting to be reassigned - not collected - but consolidated to a pension fund.

Most taxation departments offer a free online service to locate and consolidate lost pension schemes. You don't need to pay for this service. It's well worth the effort.

I know of a couple in their late 40s who found over $47,000 *each,* spread across several pension schemes!

That's money they didn't realise they had.

Pre-retirement (55+)

If you started your family at 35, by the time you hit your 50s, your children will be hitting their 20s. You have probably paid off your mortgage.

This age group has the most *disposable income* and if you missed out on travel in your 20s you are probably going to see the world in your 50s and 60s. Plus you can afford to travel in comfort. And *that* is a booming industry.

If you were sensible you also started planning for retirement in your early 40s at the very latest. However, most people put off planning until *late* 40s. As a result most people will be forced to work until their early 70s because they cannot afford to retire.

Retirement and old age (70 plus)

Hopefully, you've earned and saved enough to support yourself and your lifestyle in your retirement and old age when health and aged care are sure to become a priority.

An emerging trend will be *Baby Boomer*s downsizing to much smaller homes and/or moving into aged care. *Boomers* are already funding their retirement this way via equity loans.

This is already impacting housing prices.

We're living longer but we are not staying as healthy due to obesity, diabetes, cancer, heart disease and other illnesses. It appears you might need to also factor in the cost of health care.

And that's how the experts predict your life unfolding *financially*. Knowing this is *highly predictable* should encourage you to consider your needs going forward.

For most it doesn't.

Aas you read on you will learn capabilities and skills that will enable you to take charge of every stage of your life.

Time To Put The Book Down For A Minute

I suggest you reread the last section because a) there's a lot to to absorb; and b) it can be unsettling to see life this way.

This will make sense to much older readers who might be conscious of or nervous about financial security. But I don't expect younger readers to *emotionally* connect with these concerns just yet. But you should still be aware that these are predictable trends that most likely will affect your life, sooner or later.

And if you are a *Millennial* and this far into the book, then it suggests you are quite mature for your age!

In any case, no matter who you are, now take a few moments to consider what you're getting from the book so far. What's been a key takeaway; a key insight? What's landing?

Then, when you're ready join me in the next chapter for some good news.

Guess What? These Predictions Are Not Fixed In Concrete

Even though these stages are *statistically* typical, none of these predictions are fixed in concrete. Your life might go differently.

But the common thread through *any* stage of life however is: *do I have enough money?*

Most likely, you will be focusing on the stage you are in right now. Asking a young adult to plan for retirement that seems a long way off, might feel too unreal and so, probably doesn't make any sense right now.

But smart people start thinking about money management sooner. And they plan ahead. And even doing something as simple as forming the habit of saving 10% of your after-tax, take home income will have a positive benefit in the future.

I first learned the concept of save 10% of your after-tax, take home, income from George Clason who wrote the *The Richest Man In Babylon,* which is now a money classic.

I *still* save at least 10% of my after-tax income and therefore I *always* have money. But for many people saving is not yet a habit and having surplus cash is not yet even a goal.

I'm going to suggest that you try it. Save 10% of your take home pay for the next three months so that you start to get a sense that saving money and planning ahead is possible and beneficial ... for you.

Those people who *financially* navigate each of the stages of life well, believe it's possible, and have developed capabilities and skills, and habits in earning, spending (budgeting), saving (creating surplus), investing (leveraged spending) and giving.

And they have learned to monitor their income, set goals and targets, monitor their spending, budget where needed, planning, and importantly, take consistent action.

Even small plans and actions can yield satisfying results. The key difference between those with enough money and those without enough money – lucky windfalls aside – is knowing how much is *enough*. And then taking appropriate action even if that involves discipline and sacrifices.

Learning how to manage your money is the skill that will have the most positive impact on your entire life. Specifically, spending less, saving more and getting out of debt faster.

I recently read of a couple who had racked up credit card debts of over £41,000. To them credit card debt was considered *normal*.

Using principles outlined in this book, they reduced that debt to zero. But make no mistake, it took 22 months of smart thinking, discipline, hard work and at times, going without.

I recently chatted with a young couple, with £9,000 in credit card, who over six months managed to become debt-free.

"For a long time we ignored the problem. Eventually, we accepted we were in trouble and could no longer ignore the obvious. But the stress of the debt had to get *really* bad before we were finally motivated to even look at a website on money management.

"What shocked us was how much useful information had been *freely available* to us *at any time*. But we were the victim of our poor attitudes to money, bad habits and poor skills. And we didn't want to know."

The point is your future is highly predictable; and bad money habits come with a high price tag. Learning and applying good money habits and skills can change your entire life for the better. Spend less. Save more. Get out debt faster.

You need to know what works; and how to apply what works. Critically, you have to be ready and willing to change.

I wonder if you are? You don't have to, but ...

THE MONEY CHIMP

Money Tip #3
Make Your Money, Make *More* Money

Quick review. The top money tips so far are:

1. Spend less than you earn. Or: Don't spend more than you earn or can afford to repay; and
2. Plan for the future.

So money tip #3.

It *is* true that money makes more money but only under certain conditions. For example, reckless gambling or buying a lottery ticket may not yield any result whatsoever and can even leave you worse off.

The four proven *money makes more money* methods that work reliably are *cash, shares, property* and *businesses*.

Several years ago I had $10,000 in a bank savings account, that, after 12 months earned me $3.06 in interest. That pathetic return didn't even buy a coffee!

If I had millions to park in a bank I'd carefully pick something with a much better rate of return than 0.001%. Banks *used to be* the place to save money but right now, savers are not rewarded for leaving their hard earned money in a low interest bearing, personal savings account.

In 1982, when first married, I saved up $7,000 for the deposit on a house. We paid $18,000 for our first home. Four years later, in 1986, it sold it for $65,000. After I repaid the mortgage I had $54,000 equity and bought a home for $99,000 which later sold in 1989, for $151,000.

Maybe I'm from the generation that feels safer with bricks and mortar but property has always been a good investment for me.

Globally, there has been what's termed a *bull run* on property for over 20 years which experts say cannot continue. This means the returns you expect from property might not be as high in the future.

I know of a young man that loves shares. He bought his first share portfolio in his early 20s and his portfolio has steadily grown over time.

I love businesses. It's my favourite money making vehicle. Where else can you take seed capital of $500 and turn that into $32,000? It took a year, but that accurately describes my very first business.

Apparently, *Millennials* are quite entrepreneurial and like businesses, too. I ran a money-managing workshop with a group of young adults and most of their questions were about starting a business.

But while they might have a *good idea* for a business, it seems very few have a *good business* for the idea. We know this because 80% of business start-ups fail within the first two years; and poor financial literacy is often a key factor.

I wrote a book called *Starting!* that shows you how to stress test the assumptions in your business idea *before* you start trading. If you've already started a business, it's even more highly recommended reading. (It's available on *Amazon*.)

But you don't need to start a full-blown business. It can be part time hobby business. A project or side hustle.

At one time, I was buying and selling old books on *eBay*. I found a first-edition Enid Blyton *Noddy* book for £4 and sold it on *eBay* for £80. Some people make very good money buying and selling on *eBay, Nextdoor, Gumtree, Facebook Market* and even *Craig's List*, but you need to know exactly what you are doing.

One of the attendees at a money workshop liked the idea of buying low then selling higher. He started selling *X-Box* and *PlayStation* games on *Facebook*. He would buy them for a few pounds and on-sell them for £15 to £20 each.

Clearly there's more to *make money, make more money* – it's a book in itself.

I want to emphasise that my little $500 investment in a business wasn't a gamble. I knew *exactly* what I needed to do to leverage $500. It was not wishful thinking.

And the little house I bought, that was well-researched first, certainly paid dividends.

But that's the key point. You need to educate yourself. You have to know what you are doing. You may need to learn new skills that work. Or form new habits.

I know you don't need this book to tell you the obvious. Most people I meet *know* they need to sort out their finances. They need to think and behave differently around money.

And they fully *intend to* get cracking. But they don't.

So, why don't they? Because they run into two obstacles.

Two Big Show Stoppers

Two key roadblocks to taking action and effectively managing your money are *legitimate obstacles* and *self-imposed limitations*.

#1 Legitimate obstacles

There are several *legitimate* reasons why some people cannot manage their finances.

Some people have diminished physical or mental capacity.

Joel is 29 and profoundly disabled. He is simply incapable of managing pocket money let alone reading a bank statement.

Other people are coping with difficult circumstances such as downturns in the economy and being made redundant through industry closures (such as mining or steel works).

Others live in poor countries or face living with war or natural disasters.

My great-grandfather was a house painter and when the local coal mines shut down no one had money to spend especially on home decorating. He moved from Yorkshire to London to find work, and did, but those who stayed behind fell into abject, intergenerational poverty.

If anything like that sounds similar to your experience, then you probably *will* struggle to manage your finances.

However, there are countless stories of people who overcame incredible odds and succeeded.

#2 Self-imposed limitations

Most experts say that your ability to manage money can be diminished by self-imposed limitations. Usually limiting beliefs. For whatever reason you have convinced yourself that you're *no good with money*.

You can of course change the way you think about money at any time. Wealth coaches routinely help people change their circumstances by changing their core beliefs, skills and behaviours.

Family influences

There is a TV show in the UK called *Life On Benenfits*. It's about people who are second and third generation welfare recipients.

The people featured in the programme are usually angry at someone. It's not their fault.

They blame the government. They blame rich people. They blame other welfare recipients. But mostly they blame their own family.

Often they say things like, "The reason I'm broke is because my mum and dad were always broke."

And while they have a long list of who to blame, often they are not on their own list.

But not everyone with these circumstances, blames their parents or their upbringing or sees a hopeless future of being *broke like mum and dad.'*

I recently met a successful young entrepreneur who said, "The reason I'm wealthy is *because my mum and dad were always broke.*"

Same circumstances, different outcome. You might have to change your beliefs and work hard. You have options.

The point is everyone has values, beliefs, attitudes, skills and habits about money they learned growing up.

I grew up in a family that did not have much money. If I wanted to buy something I had to first decide if I really *needed it* or just *wanted it*. My parents asked, "Andrew, do you *need it* or *want it?*"

If I wanted it ... *I had to first explain why I needed it.* If I proved that I *needed* it then I worked for pocket money, saved up or paid it off in installments. That's how I bought my first bike. This is a lesson in delayed gratification, and a lesson I learned quite young. But how I appreciated and enjoyed my bicycle when I finally got it!

Our family didn't take bank loans, borrow money or use credit cards.

My grandparents lived through World War 1, and along with their children – my parents - they lived through the Great Depression of the early 1930s and then World War 2 in the 1940s. My parents then came through Post-War 1950s UK with food stamps and rations. They had a better time in the 1960s but then struggled through the recession of the 1970s.

So, I am sure a lot of their worries about money rubbed off on me when I was growing up!

Even though the Second World War was at least 15 years over, when I was a child, we had to eat *everything* on our plate (including the pattern). There was no dessert until we did. We were taught not to waste anything.

And there were no snacks or fast food treats in between meals.

My kids say, I still eat like I'm on post-war rations!

As I learned though, in many cultures, it's polite to *leave* some food on your plate. It actually suggests you appreciate the meal, you are satisfied but have had enough. A clean plate suggests gluttony. And greed. So, it's important to review and perhaps revisit childhood beliefs and automatic behaviours.

I am very sure you have influences that underpin your relationship with money that need reviewing.

Leading UK money coach, Fanny Snaith, takes her clients through an activity called *Your Money Story,* not dissimilar to Maria Nemeth's *Your Money Autobiography*. Both explore your historical relationship with money starting with earliest childhood memories, that in all likelihood, have shaped and continue to steer your relationship with money today. Your money story connects the dots on your early memories to your current relationship with money.

By the time I became a parent, the economy had stabilised. My adult children have no concerns about spending money. They buy whatever they want, when they want.

And they throw stuff away. And even though *I now have enough money,* I am still very careful about what I buy and throw away. In fact, to the amusement and perhaps embarrassment of my children, I sell old unwanted stuff on *eBay* rather than throw it away or donate it.

My friend, Ken the financial advisor says there are two types of investors: those who invest because of *fear* (fear of losing what they've got) and those who invest because of *optimism* and opportunities (excitement about gaining more.) I'm clearly the former.

But I admire a famous entrepreneur who said he had two goals in life: *one to make his fortune* and the other *to double it*.

I grew up believing if you wanted something, you worked for it. But the people in the TV show living on welfare *resent* that they have to even work for money. They have this accute sense of entitlement. They believe the government owes them a living. They *want* a handout. And they argue that if you grow up in that environment it is impossible to change that mind-set, or live differently. If you say so.

Your money mind-set or *software*

As we just said, you develop your mind-set about money at an early age. In a sense, when you were a kid you wrote some mental *life software* on how money works.

In most cases, you haven't upgraded your software for years or ever! Most likely, you are still running very old mental software.

You wouldn't run *Windows 4* or *OS 3* if your computer requires a more recent operating system, right? If you've got money worries it can infer your internal *money software* is due for an upgrade!

Maybe you've downloaded *someone else's* money software - like your parents - you just think it's yours!

My parents were most emphatic: *Don't waste money*. They believed borrowing money from a bank was risky. But they grew up during the 1930s Depression and a World War.

My mum at 80, lived in fear of being sent to the *workhouse*. But when she was a girl workhouses no longer even existed! That's what her parents feared! Is it any wonder that *I hate wasting money* and err on the side of financial caution?

Again, that's why most wealth coaches will ask you to write a *money autobiography* that explores the messages, rules and even admonitions you received as a child. And trust me, you *do* have a money mind-set. We all do.

Let's test that out.

What Is Money?

This is a great activity you can do yourself using the voice recorder App on your smart phone. You need to record your answers so you can listen back to them later.

Turn on the recorder and answer this one question:

What is money?

Keep asking *that same* question over and over; and record the answers as they come up.

You need money. Money is stressful. Money is for rich people.

I once did this activity for over two hours and was surprised and sometimes shocked at what beliefs are sitting just below the surface. Even a short exposure to this simple activity will give you an indication of your current *money software.*

That software might include fears and attitudes that translate into limiting beliefs such as *There's not enough to go round; Be careful with money; You are bad if you waste money; Easy come easy go; You can have anything you want; If you love me you will spend money on me* and so on.

There are thousands of beliefs we form about money as

children *that continue to influence us as adults.* A lot of them are inaccurate and well past their used-by date.

By flushing out these old beliefs you will identify beliefs that work and the ones you need to change.

Many people believe they are *no good at managing money and never will be*. But this is totally false. In fact, it's a lie. Anyone can learn financial skills and be responsible with money at *any time* and *any age.*

Even you.

Right?

OK, I'm Stuck

Now, if you believe there is *absolutely nothing* you can do to change your financial lot, then understand, it means you *are* highly committed. To that option. *Just the wrong option*.

But once that happens you now have an excuse for inaction! There is no point to even bother trying to manage your money wisely. Why?

We all act on what we believe to be true. If you believe you are hopeless with money then there will always be *more month than money*. And you will then procrastinate and abdicate responsibility. You might promise yourself to sort it *one day*. You believe things will only be better as soon *as you get a pay rise*, or a new job, or win the lottery or get an inheritance.

You might fantasise that next Friday night you will win the $133 million lottery jackpot. And that Father Christmas, the tooth fairy and a luck genie all back your plan.

This is the standard profile of a *spender*.

By the way, most people who win the lottery are broke within 18 months, because while their financial circumstances change, their beliefs, attitudes and thinking - and mental software - don't. Most winners spend their millions or give it away to family and friends.

Very few invest. And most end up in worse debt.

Wealth coach, Karen Sutton-Johal understands debt better than most. She says that her childhood was essentially one financial disaster after another. That inspired her to become a debt adviser. She noticed that people who get out of debt will go straight back into debt simply because they don't change their money mind-set. A wealth coach will challenge your beliefs. In most cases once your mind-set changes you will start managing your money a lot better.

If you say things like, *I can't get my head around money* or *I can't learn this* or *I'm no good at budgeting* a money coach will ask, *Because ... ?* to check if your reasons are legitimate, self-imposed or just *old software*. Understand: saying *I can't* usually means you need to give yourself permission to change.

UK life strategist, Kain Ramsay says you are the only person who can do that. Only you can be responsible for your life.

When you say things like *I can't ...* or *I'm no good at ...* you are not taking responsibility. Spenders ultimately behave irresponsibly. I'm sorry but managing your money requires that you take on responsibility. But spenders wish that life was different ... and then *behave as if it were.*

UK money saving expert, Martin Lewis says that most people simply need to make better choices. He believes we are far too loyal to *existing suppliers.* Lewis says, "You are most likely paying too much for everything! *Shop around!* You will be stunned at just how much money you can save. Every little *does* help."

This is a brilliant way to think about managing your money, as well.

As one US money coach sums up, "Money isn't just about having a head for figures. It's about understanding your beliefs and behaviours and the unconscious inheritance you've received from people and events in the past. All of that can change for the better."

So, Let's Talk About Credit Cards

I am big fan of credit cards ... when they are used as originally intended as a short-term, interest-free line of credit; and paid in full by the due date. I use my credit card wisely and I usually pay off the balance when it falls due and pay zero interest charges.

But most people don't use their credit card wisely, don't pay off the amount when due, needlessly incur excess interest, late fees and charges and end up with crippling credit card debt. Subsequently, Brits owed a staggering £72.5bn on credit cards of which young professionals owe £9.7bn.

I recently read about a 29-year old executive who racked up £50,000 on credit cards. Can you even imagine getting a bank statement that says you owe £50,000 on your credit card? And given that the *Annual Percentage Rate* (APR) was 27%, can you see how fast she was going into long-term chronic debt?

It was manageable until one day she was made redundant and then like a house of cards her world fell apart. She divorced, lost her home and her car was repossessed. In the end, she declared bankruptcy.

As an exercise she analysed 24 months of statements to see *exactly* what she'd spent £50,000 on. It came down to buying the latest gadgets and the latest designer label clothing and accessories.

And the key driver was to impress others.

Access to credit

Did you know that in the early 1970s women could not get a loan or a credit card without their father or husband giving permission or acting as guarantor?

That all changed with the introduction of laws like the *Equal Pay* and *Sex Discrimination Acts of 1975* (UK). But …

But, are men are better at managing money? No, the ability to manage money is not gender specific. It's a skill both genders can and should master. Men get into chronic debt just as quickly and easily as women.

Impulse control

Access to credit has overridden two important psychological drivers; *impulse control* and the *ability to delay gratification*. This is what we are trying to teach children when we toilet train them, teach them to do homework before television, or eat their vegetables before they have dessert. Impulse says *I want it now!* and *I do not want to wait*.

We know about this because Stanford University conducted a landmark study in the 1960s that became known as *The Marshmallow Test*.

Experimenters sat four year olds in a room at a table with a lolly and a bell and said, "If you can wait 15 minutes you can have *two* lollies. But if you want one lolly, right now, ring the bell." And then left the room. And that's a tough challenge for any four year old.

Here's what happened.

A lot of kids rang the bell straight away and ate the lolly. Other kids resisted for a short time and then ate the lolly. But some kids found ways to *not* eat the lolly. They distracted themselves. They sang songs or looked away. And after what must have seemed an eternity, *they got two lollies!*

Those children were then surveyed over the next 20 years. The kids that *waited* were more successful in *all* endeavours of life than the kids that couldn't wait.

By the way, at no time were parents or participants made aware of their performance.

This experiment is *culturally robust* and over time meaning whenever and wherever this experiment is conducted in the world they *still* get a similar result.

But a credit card is like saying, *Here's the lolly. Don't wait. Eat it now. Pay later.*

Credit cards give you the power to let you have what you want - *now!* And that feels good.

In fact, the brain has a reward system called the mesolimbic pathway that releases the dopamine hormone that make us feel good when we engage in certain activities. The problem is spending money feels good and credit cards let you spend a lot more than you ever intended.

Basically, the science confirms it is hard to say *No* when it feels good to say *Yes*.

So a wealth coach will help you identify how you spend money on your credit card, how you can use it more wisely and hopefully how to stay debt-free in the process. But will you want to? Not at first.

But the message is clear: you must learn to delay gratification and control your impulse to spend. That requires awareness.

I like credit cards and use them to pay for a range of things like fuel, train tickets, meals and so on. But I pay the balance when it falls due so I take full advantage of 55 days interest-free credit. And I have good cash flow. It only works because I pay off the credit card when it falls due each month.

But what if you can't pay it all off?

A simple idea when reducing credit card debt is to focus on the smallest debts first, and get rid of those. For example, I took three months to pay off an airline ticket but paid all the minor charges off on time.

Some wealth experts say the best way to reduce credit card debt is to stop using your credit card. They suggest putting your credit card in the freezer! If you think that is necessary, then try it.

Best-selling author and money expert, Diana Mathew advocated a much stronger remedy: *cut them up!* I am not advocating either method but I *am* suggesting you find out how you historically use your credit card; and what it costs you.

You need to know your spending patterns.

But if you can't manage your impulse to spend, then maybe Diana Mathew is right: cut up your credit cards and stop incurring more debt.

Listen To Your Money Talk

When I listen to people talk about money they either *sound like a kid* or they *sound like a grown up*. Have you noticed?

If people say things like, *I can't … I haven't … I must… I should … it's too late … money is so boring … I hate saving … I just wanna… I'm helpless… I'm no good … I don't want to … yes but … I'm scared to look … why are we doing this anyway? … I've got to … you can't make me* - and with a helpless, whiny tone - then typically this is someone who is emotionally young and immature in the way they think about money.

And they usually act helpless and even scared when asked to think about being more responsible with money.

Regardless of their chronological age when the topic turns to saving or budgeting they go child-like. They glaze over and the shutters come down. They resist. Or rebel.

Just watch any *YouTube* video of cops dealing with entitled brats who think life is unfair when they get arrested for breaking the law.

Suddenly, very smart people feel overwhelmed and find it hard to concentrate. If you are over 18 - legally an adult and responsible for your actions - *and you sound like this*, then you have a problem.

If someone says, *I'm learning this ... I'm trying that ... I'm reading about ... I asked someone about ... I did a course ... I'm talking to my bank ... I set up ... I read my statements ... I'm learning how ... this is interesting ... I'll give that a go ... I plan to ...* then typically I am talking to someone who is more grown-up around money.

By the way, I haven't said *adult* on purpose.

It has little to do with your chronological age. The ability to manage your money is a *grown-up* skill. If it were an *adult* skill then all adults would manage their money wisely. But I know a lot of adults with chronic or serious money problems. And I know children who can manage their pocket money better than their parents.

Pay close attention to the *energy*. The trick is to consider - *energetically* - whether you *feel* more like a kid or a grown-up around money, regardless of your chronological age.

Managing money is *grown ups* work.

If you sense you are *feeling* like a kid - helpless, victimised, overwhelmed - then shut your eyes, take a few deep breaths and quietly repeat these magic words, *This is grown-ups work. This is grown-ups work.* You will *feel* your *energy* and your thinking shift to a more resourceful state.

Guaranteed.

Part 2

The Five Habits
And Five Skills

THE MONEY CHIMP

Is Managing Your Money A Science Or An Art?

It's both. Money works along fixed principles that are so easy to understand and start using that anyone as young as an 10 year old can get it right. The money managing principles in this book are time-tested, proven and established.

We know *exactly* what works. For example:

Don't spend more than you earn.

And while increasing your income and controlling your spending is important, there are eight other principles.

If you follow these principles and apply them, then in most cases, you will be financially better off, within 90 days.

But here's the bad news.

While the principles are easy to understand they may require some smart thinking and hard work to start implementing.

Why?

Because it might involve changing long-standing, ingrained habits, attitudes and beliefs; and developing new skills. Changing anything requires conscious effort and usually requires you to get uncomfortable.

How you do money is how you do life. But the way you are with money right now is nothing more than a habit. And habits are just that – activities you've done over and over again until they are automatic. The problem is many of those habits are well past their use-by date and based on information that was probably well out-of-date when you first learned it.

If you are in debt and doing nothing about it then you are saying, *I'm no good at managing money and my only option is to remain in debt.*

But there's one big problem with such a limiting option.

If you believe you are no good at managing money then you *now* have a good excuse for doing nothing. You will unconsciously decide not to look for other options. Why learn how to manage your money? Or how to be cashed-up and debt-free? You'll argue, *I'm no good at managing money.* So, why even try?

But you *do* have other options and that involves making mature decisions and proactive, positive choices.

Learning new skills takes commitment, right? But right now you already *are* committed! You are just committed to the wrong thing - mismanaging your money and being in debt! You're committed to the wrong strategy!

This book gives you ten proven money managing principles that work, that are easy to understand and that you can use starting right away. Right now, today. Let me show you:

- Two sisters – both university students - were both debt-free in 90 days after applying just a little bit of what they learned.

- A drummer with a rock band was debt-free within 90 days after applying what he learned here.

- An unemployed 19-year old on minimum wage of $4.27 per hour went on to create a little business that earns him $15 per hour, 8 hours a day, 5 days a week.

- A youth pastor went from being perpetually broke to bringing his finances under control within 90 days.
- A high-income earning doctor went from massive debt to finances under control within six months.
- A husband and wife of 30 years reduced their discretionary spending by £1,200 a month! Ironically, both worked as financial advisors!
- A couple with over £41,000 in credit card debts were debt-free within 22 months.
- A single mum with $8,000 in credit card debt was debt-free within 200 days.

While there is no guarantee you will be debt-free in 90 days, the ten principles in this book will prove helpful in moving you closer to that goal - sooner as long as you do something like applying the simple suggestions in this book.

While this book is not intended to resolve serious financial problems within 90 days - like being £41,000 in debt - using these principles in conjunction with professional advice will certainly move you in the right direction, sooner.

These people were all making some of the Top ten mistakes. They all made a committed and sincere 90-day test of the ideas in this book. It did not require affirmations or the adoption of some nonsensical belief system. It required developing new skills and applying them.

They learned the ten principles and then took action.

Most success was built on taking small steps. In some cases, drastic measures. But ultimately, they could see the steps they needed to take ... *and they took them.*

I propose to show you the top ten money managing mistakes that you are making and then explain what to do to fix those problems. But first ...

THE MONEY CHIMP

Your Performance Plan

If you want to improve *anything* in your life there are three things that consistently work:

- You have to **STOP** doing what doesn't work
- You have to change and **START** doing what does work; and
- You have to **CONTINUE** doing things that are working.

Change is required in each step.

A university student, Melanie, had to STOP running up credit card debt buying fashion, accessories, shoes, handbags and expensive beauty treatments, essentially, to impress her friends.

Melanie had to START to reduce her £9,000 credit card debt. She STARTED to get serious about reducing debt by taking a second job to fast track that result. That second job was part-time, two nights a week on Fridays and Saturdays.

Obviously, her social life took a nose dive for a while.

And she had to CONTINUE that new habit. This became so much easier once she saw the credit card debt reducing.

Once she got the credit card debt under control she had to CONTINUE doing what she was doing to keep it that way.

You might *relapse*. Relapse means going right back to the very habit that needed to be changed such as racking up credit card debt on fashion.

Relapse is actually highly predictable when you are trying to change any habit. Expect setbacks. Normalise it.

If you want to read a brilliant book on changing just about anything, read *Changing for Good*. Prochanska, Norcross and Diclemente's ground breaking research has been at the forefront of change for the last 40 years specifically as it applies to people with addictions. They say: *expect relapse*. Expecting *relapse* can help you avoid it, because you expect it. Or at the very least accept that relapse is now considered a normal part of change.

I also asked Melanie to reflect on where she got the idea that *treating herself* required expensive shopping expeditions. Turns out it's a *social thing* linked to being liked and approved of by her friends.

My client Troy runs a successful construction business but has an expensive recreational drug habit. When we talked it through it turns out that Troy gets a lot approval from his mates mainly because he is usually the one buying the drugs.

He says if he gives up drugs he won't get to party with his mates. Of course, there is also the addictive nature of the substance. But, when Troy stepped in front of a fast moving taxi late one night none of his so-called *mates* came to see him in hospital. Nor did they chip in for his medical bills.

At the heart of your problems with managing money are your beliefs about money. Here's proof.

What Is Money ... Again?

Hey, didn't we already do this activity? I am guessing if you are like most people you promised to go back to it or skipped it altogether. So, here's the exercise again.

Again, you need a voice recorder and you need to record your answers. You can of course write them down but I've found recording your answers works much better especially because I want you to listen back to this recording later.

Just keep asking yourself the *same* question: *what is money?* And keep answering with whatever first comes to mind:

What is money? Money is ...

Try it right now. Answer the question.

- *What is money?* Money is struggle.
- *What is money?* Money is fun.
- *What is money?* Money is about paying bills.
- *What is money?* Money is going to pay for something and my card is declined.

Get the idea? Just keep going.

Just say the first thing that comes to mind. I am sure you will find both positive and negative beliefs. The trick is not to give up too soon. Some people do this activity for about three minutes and then say, *OK, I get it. I have some stupid beliefs about money. Next!*

But don't stop. Keep going. Persist.

What is money? Money is ...

The benefit comes in persisting.

I first learned this activity at a money workshop and have done this activity with many people since. People can easily feel discouraged at first but as they continue with the exercise they gain powerful insights. They hear their fears and beliefs out loud.

By the way, this is a great activity to do with a trusted friend. Your friend, however, should *not* engage you in a discussion. They should just listen and let you talk and only ask, *What is money?* Just ask that question only.

This activity is designed to uncover your money mind-set.

If you want to read two books on money mind-set I suggest you read *The Energy of Money* by Maria Nemeth PhD - which you will find refreshingly challenging - and *Coach Yourself to Wealth* by Shirley McKinnon. I also suggest you read *The Money Tree* by Diana Mathew who managed to dig herself out from under a mountain of debt by first changing the way she thought about money.

Melanie uncovered several childish fears such as she was helpless, would never be good with money and that someone else should take care of her money worries. "It was really useful listening back to the recording and hearing myself say these things out loud."

But what if you want a precise snapshot of you money issues?

Take *The Money Chimp* Quiz

I'm hoping you are starting to realise that the better you understand *your* current money managing habits and skills the more likely you are to develop more resourceful habits and skills that lead to more positive results. I'm about to share a tool that will give you a clear heads up and fast track everything I am saying so far.

It's called the *Money Chimp* test.

It is an inexpensive online test that takes about seven minutes to complete. You answer 35 questions. Then you get back a personalised, 20-page report of your money managing habits and skills, plus specific recommendations.

Here's that link: *www.moneychimp.net*

The test and report costs a small amount of money. But this test will save you a lot of wasted time and money in the future.

People who have taken *The Money Chimp* test say:

"I am a financial planner and *The Money Chimp* test is accurate and bang on target. Brilliant."

Ken, Financial Advisor

"It was frighteningly accurate and gave me the big wake-up call I needed to sort out my finances."

Steven, Software designer

"The report accurately described my money managing skills, highlighted blind spots and gave practical recommendations."

Eric, Life Skills trainer

"*The Money Chimp* report totally grabbed the attention of my 19 and 25 year olds. It was totally accurate."

Mark, Father of two young adults

"Me and my girlfriend loved the book and did the test. The book made so much more sense because we could then relate *our* skills to each section."

Tim and Sarah, Young couple 26 and 25

Let's now look at the top ten money managing habits and skills.

The Top 10 Money Managing Principles

I conducted an extensive review of books, courses, websites and literature on money management. As I expected the key topics covered income, expenditure, assets and liabilities.

But I clearly identified five money activities - *earning, spending, saving, investing* and *giving*; and five money managing skills - *monitoring, focusing, reducing, developing* and *taking action*.

The Five Money Activities

- **Earn** more than enough income to meet your needs.
- **Spend** less than you earn (and know your liabilities)
- **Save** money (pay yourself first, save 10% of everything you earn, save for emergencies, plan for the future)
- **Invest** (in assets, pensions, property etc).
- **Give** money to reputable charities.

The Five Money Managing Skills

- **Monitor** your income and expenditure and savings and investments.
- **Focus** and have clear financial plans
- **Reduce** wasteful, superfluous or unnecessary spending and expenses.
- **Develop** your money managing skills and financial literacy. And;
- **Take action and apply** what you are learning.

People who struggle with money make these top ten mistakes:

- **Not earning enough** (when you can earn more).
- **Spending more than you earn** and wasting money. This also includes spending *borrowed* money you can't repay and racking up huge credit card debts.
- **Not saving any money** for bills, emergencies, holidays, birthdays, Christmas gifts etc.
- **Not investing money** wisely or at all.
- **Not giving**.
- **Not monitoring** what you earn, spend, save, invest or give.
- **Not focusing on your financial goals or targets.**
- **Not reducing** expenditure when it's obvious you need to
- **Not developing** your money managing skills or financial literacy.
- **Not applying** what you are learning.

Read this section again.

Time To Review

I suggest you reread the top ten money managing principles. Which of the habits and skills sound *most* like you? What are you already doing well and where do you need the most help?

And what are you learning so far? What's making sense? What key insights are you getting about the way you manage money, so far?

If you apply even a small amount of the recommendations in this book you will start to see an improvement in your personal finances and your ability to manage your money.

So, I'm now going to explore each of the five money activities and five money managing skills in more detail and give you some practical ideas to try out. These practical ideas genuinely work, but be warned, they will not work if you don't try them.

So, we'll start by exploring the five money activities.

Part 3

The Five Money Activities

THE MONEY CHIMP

Money Activity #1 Earning

The reality is most people *do* earn enough money. But most people *spend* more than they earn each month. We use the *monthly* time period because that's how most debt advisors and banks assess your ability to manage money and repay loans.

Even if you don't have a loan, start thinking how much it costs you to live - on average - *per calendar month*. We will also explore what you typically spend your money on *per month*.

For now, on average, how much money do you *earn per month?*

Earnings is another name for *income*. Importantly, if you are an employee and wage earner, you need to know your *exact* take-home pay, *after-tax* (income).

Ask your boss or pay manager to provide you with a *pay advice slip* which will show your gross earnings; the total amount of take-home pay; the total amount of periodic *variable* deductions (deductions that can change from payday to payday such as *National Insurance (NI)* and tax); and *fixed* deductions (deductions that don't change from payday to payday such as union fees, pension contributions etc.).

A pay slip also includes your tax code, NI number, pay rate (annual and per hourly rate); and additional payments such as overtime, tips and bonuses.

Please note, it is recommended that you get a current pay advice slip and that you read and understand it. I recently spoke to someone who thought their pay rate was £10.55 per hour but in fact they were being paid at £7.33 per hour. That created a dilemma - *do I say anything to my boss?*

A lot of wage earners I meet do not have this basic information at hand. And if they do, they don't read it carefully. Or rarely is it current.

You might receive a pay advice slip with the regular pay. But its worthless if you don;t actually take the time to know what's on that pay slip.

I can tell you that current Employment Laws in most countries tell us that the employer should give you a current pay advice slip. But an employment law colleague said he was stunned that far too many employees do not have this basic information to hand or at all.

If you are an employee ask your boss for a pay advice slip.

Three Sources Of Income

In addition to knowing how much you earn each month, it's important to know the *source* of that money.

Most tax departments segment income into three key sources:

- **Earned income** - salaries or self-employed income
- **Non-earned income** - pensions, benefits, dividends and annuities, bank interest, reimbursements
- **Other sources of income** - winnings, gifts etc.

So, the tip here is to start identifying the *source* of your income.

If you earn a wage, the source of income is typically *earned income*. If you receive bank interest that's deemed *non-earned income* – but its still income. If you win £1,000 on the lottery, technically, you have to declare that as income and pay tax on it. But, it would come under *other* income.

Sometimes, I get asked about *reimbursements*. Let's say your boss asks you to buy coffees for the team and you pay for it with your cash or on your credit card.

Or, say you use a company car for a work related purpose and need to refuel that vehicle but you pay for the fuel on your credit card. Well you want to be reimbursed, right?

Your employer will reimburse the amount back to you but

they usually ask for a receipt to reimburse the correct sum. So, if you want to be reimbursed, whenever you purchase anything while on the job, *get a receipt!* Then give it to your employer, immediately, so you can be reimbursed.

Obviously, you wouldn't need to declare that as a source of income because *you've* already earned and paid tax on that money. You don't want to pay tax twice.

However, if you are self-employed you might be required to show *all* expenses *and reimbursements* in your bookkeeping and maybe even on invoices.

Talk to an accountant or book keeper.

But employee or self-employed, start asking for receipts.

Earn More Than 'Just Enough'

Your goal isn't to earn just *enough* money to cover your monthly living expenses. Your goal is to do better than that! The goal is to create *surplus cash*.

Most people are about two or three pay days away from financial trouble and about two to three months from chronic debt, serious money hassles and even personal bankruptcy (RBS 2012, 2016).

Crisis, the UK homeless charity says some independent young adults are one month away from homelessness! That might be a bit dramatic but having volunteered for several years at their annual *Crisis at Christmas* event, and heard the stories firsthand, I am sad to say it can be a likelihood for some.

So here are three goals:

- Your first goal is to work out how much you earn per annum *and* per calendar month.

- Then, you need to add up your expenses - what you spend, on average, on monthly bills and see if you have *more money than month* or *more month than money*. It may take you several weeks to work out your total average monthly commitments.

- Next, you should start setting aside some money for unexpected bills and financial emergencies (see *Spending*).

Carol had to pay a $2,000 veterinary bill and that money had to come from somewhere. Fortunately, she had set money aside for emergencies and had the money.

She went back over the last 24 months and reviewed all the *unexpected* bills she paid. She calculated that she needed about $3,000 in cash reserves – to be safe – just to cover *unexpected* stuff.

Carol sets aside $60 a week in her *emergency fund*. Some years she doesn't spend anywhere near $3,000 on emergencies but it's there just in cas*e*.

As it turns out $3,000/£2,000 is about the right amount for most people.

But most people have *nothing* set aside for even a small emergency such as an unexpected car repair or a dental bill.

The next goal is a biggie.

Have at least three to six months worth of monthly living expenses in cash reserves

Top UK investment coach, Jason Graystone suggests having between three to six months living expenses in cash reserves. It's called a *liquidity cushion* or *financial buffer*.

I injured my back and was off work for three months with no pay. And it took another ten weeks before I was working full time. But I had saved up six months worth of living expenses and that's how we got through those 13 weeks.

Let's pretend your living expenses are £2,000 PCM. Three months means you'd need to save up £6,000. Six months means £12,000. The best way to do this is to create a special bank account just for your *cash reserve fund* … and start saving. Even if its a little, save up and don't spend it.

Finally:

You need to save for your future retirement; and set aside at least 10% of your take home pay a year for special projects such as education and personal development

What does that look like?

Bill has a *Pension Scheme* and for every $1,000 he wants back in retirement per annum he is contributing $10,000. His goal is to have a $40,000 a year pension so he will need about $400,000 in the scheme.

Jillian wanted to attend a 12-month course. The fees were £7,500. She started saving for the course and when she enrolled she was able to pay in cash. But it got better. Because she was a cash up-front student they offered her a 20% cash discount of £1,500.

You need very clear *Earning* goals based on your current living expenses. And I'm advising you to earn enough to cover financial emergencies.

If you don't have *Earning* goals you will earn money, pay your bills and spend whatever is left over on right-here-right-now stuff. Usually fun stuff.

But we know most people over-spend ... everything

There's wisdom in the old saying *Save for a rainy day!*

Most people who do my workshops learn to earn more, spend less, save more, set aside money for rainy days and reduce their debts.

But how can you earn more? Here's some ideas:

- **Ask for a pay rise.** Most people are due a pay rise but never ask for one. An employer is *not* obliged to offer you a pay rise if you don't ask. The key to a pay rise is to be of more value. Most people don't understand this. They arrive late, watch the clock and go home early if they can. Doing the opposite makes you more valuable.

I often ask employees who they work for and they name their company or their boss. The reality is you actually work for yourself. You just happen to have one customer - your boss.

Think of yourself as an *intrapreneur* running your own business *inside* someone else's business. Your job is to be of more value at work.

But also check your pay advice slip and your pay rate. You might be under-paid! For example, the hourly pay rate is £10.55 and you're being paid £7.33.

- **Work extra shifts or better paying shifts.** You might need to sacrifice your social life for a while. Nikola worked the night shift for two years and saved up to afford a 15% deposit on a small flat.

- **Work a second job.** Craig worked a four-hour shift at his local pub two nights a week but that money built up over time and he was able to clear his credit card debt over several months.

- **Sell stuff you don't use anymore.** A drummer from a rock band sold off three drum kits that were gathering dust in his loft. Fans bought those kits as *collectibles.* And he cleared his credit card debts. Win-win!

  A 16 year-old sold his old *X-Box* and *PlayStation* games on *eBay*. Then he started selling other people's games for a small commission.

- **Start your own *side hustle* or part-time business.** Young Jake was 17 and unemployed. The best he could manage was casual work at a local fast food for $4.27 an hour. He borrowed his dad's leaf blower and a rake and offered to clean front yards of small terrace houses in his neighbourhood.

  Most houses were within 300 yards from his own home. He charged $5 for a quick cleanup and he could do three houses an hour.

Pretty soon he was making $15 an hour. That's significantly more than he was earning working in a fast food store. This is a kid with a profitable service business with most customers all within a short walk from home.

Debbie has two kids and after work she irons. She used to sit and watch TV. Now she irons and makes extra money while she watches TV. That little business started from a letter box drop in her street.

Lois is a touch typist who transcribes MP3s for legal firms. That gives her an extra £200 a week.

- **Get a better job.** Ironically, if you are of more value in your current job you can easily justify a pay-rise but sometimes you simply need to find a better job that pays more money.
- **Start your own business**. Essentially, no pay rate applies. You can get paid what you feel you are worth - or what the market can bear.

Of course, do not do anything illegal like failing to declare earnings *especially* if it is a cash-only business. It infers that the purpose of that business is to avoid paying tax.

Keep impeccable records; and seek qualified accounting advice. Stay on the right side of the law.

What can I do to increase my income? Get creative. Like Debbie, start in your own street. Russell Conwell's book *Acres of Diamonds* claims there is probably more than enough money to be made close by to where you live right now, if you look.

One final word. If you are an employee on a fixed income getting your finances under control will depend on *spending less* of what you earn and trying to *save more*. The creative way forward is to increase your earnings.

Remember Melanie who had £9,000 in credit card debts? There's no way on her wage she could have got out from under that debt by only spending less. It was only made possible by taking on an extra job. Once her debt was cleared she quit that job and by then she was much better at managing her money.

Despite having a demanding job as a teacher a friend devoted four years to paying off his student loan by working a second job.

As you might expect, the couple who owed over £41,000 had to make drastic changes – cutbacks, downsizing, eliminating all luxuries such as dining out. They also took second jobs, switched gas and electricity suppliers, sold off unwanted stuff etc.

That took a lot of discipline, sacrifice and willpower, but, after 22 months they were debt-free.

Sean was self-employed running a small cleaning company. He was able to pay off debts by selling more of his cleaning services and working longer hours for a time. But he increased his income and traded out of his debt.

I once had a $25,000 loan which I traded out of through sheer hard work; and some clever refinancing.

It is possible to be debt-free but it usually takes smart thinking and hard work. If you are frightened of hard work you will find it harder to be debt-free let alone financially free.

Another way to have more money might be to ask anyone who's borrowed money from you to repay it. Many people attending the workshop said that people owed them money. One young woman was owed £2,000 from a family member.

You can also increase your income through investing. Investments often can make more money faster than you can by working harder.

But more on that later.

Your Turn

It's time to review what you read and convert that into action steps.

- How much money do you actually earn?
- Find out where your income comes from (earned, non-earned, other)?
- What can you do increase your income?
- Re-read this chapter and brainstorm some ideas that would be easy for you to implement straight away. If you could apply what you learned in this chapter, what would that lock like? How would *you* know it was working? Take a moment to think those questions through.

Money Activity #2: Spending

In 2012, the chief economist of the *Royal Bank of Scotland* stated that most people spend 130% of their weekly income. This means that most of us are living beyond our means. This is especially true of young people (18-25 year olds).

Pretend you earn £100. It means you're spending £130. That extra money has to come from somewhere: usually your credit card.

But what are you spending that extra money on? Do you remember the section on *infographics*? Did you *Google* what householders in your country spend money on?

Here's a reminder. There's bills – taxes, rent, loans, weekly food shopping, transport, rates, utilities etc – what we call *grudge purchases*. Petrol is a grudge purchase because we *hate* spending money on it. Gas and electricity are grudge purchases. You don't ever get excited and yell, *Yippee!* when you pay your electricity bill.

Bills aside, the research suggests we waste money on stuff we don't need like botox treatments, pre-torn jeans, alcohol, cigarettes, entertaining, the very latest smart phone - all consumer goods that lose value as soon as you leave the shop.

We also get charged for *hidden* expenses such as bank fees, charges and interest. By the way, they are not actually *hidden* at all but in plain view if you read your bank statements!

You cannot avoid spending money but you need to ensure that your spending does not exceed your income. That's why you need to know your current living expenses almost down to the penny. Living expenses means what it costs you just to live, on average *per calendar month* (PCM).

Most people have a *general* idea but some people have no idea at all. You need to work this out.

Your main monthly expenses typically segment into:

- **Liabilities** – rent, mortgage, personal loans
- **Recurring bills** – rates, insurances, school fees
- **Periodic bills** – gas, electricity, water, rates etc
- **Consumer debt** – loans, credit cards and charge card payments, fees and interest charges
- **Living expenses** – food, household spending, transport, etc
- **Discretionary spending** - *fun money*. Fun money is the most wasteful. Your money disappears on simple pleasures like coffees, takeaways, dining out, social events, holidays, fashion, gadgets and gifts.

You can certainly reduce your spending in any of these categories but for a quick result start to focus on reducing *discretionary spending*.

Here's an example. Ian complains he doesn't have enough money. But he smokes. His brand costs £12.40 and he smokes five packets a week. Over a year that's £3224. Ian clearly *has* enough money to spend on cigarettes!

But does £3224 seem a lot to you? It does to me. And I can't see the point of *burning* money *and* harming your health. Ian takes home about £25,000 a year after-tax so £3224 is almost 12.9% of his take-home income!

Steven monitored what he spent on alcohol. Turns out he spends about £180 every Friday night. That's about £9,360 on alcohol a year. Steven also complains of not having *enough* money. But he clearly has enough money to spend on alcohol.

Kirsty's mobile phone plan is $35 per month ($420pa) but she loves downloading music and streaming movies and videos so her actual monthly phone bill always carries an *excess charge* and bumps it closer to $67 per month ($804). That's almost double - an additional $384.

These young people *think* they haven't got enough money but they do.

Let's say you smoke, drink *and* overuse your mobile phone. Using the above figures that's GBP£13,004 (USD$16,845 and AUD$24,739.) If your salary is £25,000 that's about half. In the UK, US *and* Australia that's also enough money for a deposit on a small apartment!

And, let's say you need £2,000 PCM living expenses. That's six months worth of living expenses in cash reserves, *right there*. The reality is most people have *enough money* but are wasting it on stuff that doesn't matter. Or worse, on stuff that damages their health.

But what else can you do with that money?

Well, I'm going to argue, pay down your debt; or invest that money in a pension scheme; or go back to university and get a qualification; or start a business. Anything, but do something much better with that money! Otherwise it's a sad waste.

By the way, I am sure tobacco, alcohol and mobile phone companies love your lack of discipline.

Start to identify *exactly* what you spend your money on each month. Get a notebook and write down *everything* you spend. Or use a spreadsheet. Or an App.

There are some great Apps for your phone like *Receipt Bank, Expense Tracker* or *Pocket Expense* that track expenses and even send you alerts if you are nudging towards breaking the budget. But I've noticed that people learn more about managing money from using the good old pen, paper and calculator.

UK money saving expert, Martin Lewis suggests that a key benefit of tracking your spending is you can start seeing ways to start making savings. He says that 70% of consumers can make significant savings on their phone, internet, utility and energy bills simply by shopping around and even switching suppliers.

Lewis says two big lessons you need to learn are 1) suppliers are in business to make money. And 2), you can and should renegotiate better tariffs or switch suppliers. He says most customers pay dearly for their loyalty by not shopping around especially on things like energy and phone and internet bills. And even bank loans.

But you can't make any savings unless you know the cost of your current plan or tariff, your usage and what you spend on average each month, quarter and year. Most people just don't know. Or cant be bothered to find out. That's an expensive choice.

So, the big recommendation is to ...

Get Receipts For Everything And Read Your Bank Statements

Emily is in her early 30s and she loves shopping. And she started collecting and reviewing receipts. After two months, she was stunned at how much she spent on coffees and takeaway lunches alone. So she cut spending on those items and started saving up for something of greater value such as a well-earned holiday. This month she is flying to India with her husband for their wedding anniversary, something they've dreamed of for several years.

You need to STOP spending everything you earn on frivolous, short-term items and START setting aside money for lasting rewards such as a well-earned holiday. Or a home deposit.

The goal is to *spend less* and *save more*. Remember: most Brits spend 130% of their weekly income!

Not so obvious are debt transactions such as credit cards, store cards, loans, borrowings, fees, late fees, charges and penalties.

Maybe in the past banks targeted young people because they racked up huge credit card debts ever so quickly. But banks have discovered while it's easy to lend money the trick is getting it back. Banks are very concerned if you look as if you are about to enter a cycle of *unpayable debt*.

I already mentioned Steven who spends an average of £180 on alcohol every Friday night. That's nearly £800 a month!

Note: he pays for those drinks on his credit card. And, he rarely pays off his credit card on time, so he gets hit with late fees and interest charges.

Alcohol is so wasteful. It's expensive. You drink it. An hour later you pee it out. And the next day you have a hangover. And we call that fun!

Most people do not pay off their entire end-of-month credit card bill on time – or even the interest-only component – so they start getting interest on interest (and this is an example of money making more money *for the banks*.)

Worse yet, some young people do not realise they are even paying interest on interest payments as soon as they miss a payment! Time goes so fast and over 12 months you would be staggered at what you've paid in interest fees alone.

I said earlier that interest payments are *hiddens* but in fact they are *not* hidden. They are in plain sight on your bank statement. But they may as well be hidden if you don't bother to read your bank statement. So learn to read statements. Read the bit that says: *Interest Paid This Month*.

Ask for receipts and always cross-check those receipts against the statements.

I once bought an item for $136 but the credit card statement showed I was actually charged $316. I hadn't even looked at the receipt issued at the point of sale and didn't pick up this error until over a month later.

After a trip to the States I discovered someone in Arizona had purchased a $1,299 laptop on my credit card. Fortunately, I had checked my statement a day or two later, phoned the bank, and the bank reimbursed that fraudulent purchase.

Your goal is to get rid of credit card and store card debt. Do whatever you can to reduce and clear any card debts. And then use your card responsibly.

The big killer can be store cards as they carry heftier APR interest fees. This is why big department stores encourage you to sign up to their loyalty card. Store cards are, of course, okay if you pay them off on time.

Our drummer didn't realise that one of his store cards was incurring 27% interest PCM. If he missed the payment he was paying interest on top of the monthly APR rate of 27%!

Once he started reading every statement carefully he started picking up details like fees, fines and interest charges and even overcharges. Read your statements.

Another money trap is your mobile phone. According to a major phone company, *Millennials* rack up massive bills on talk time, downloads, gaming, streamed content and bandwidth usage *that exceeds their monthly phone plan.*

I was on a train from London to Edinburgh and overheard a young girl chatting about new shoes she had purchased. That conversation lasted all the way from Paddington to Peterborough! Maybe she had a generous phone plan, but charges hike once you exceed the usage allowance.

A massive money pit is dining out. Emily was spending a whopping £1,200 *a month* on meeting friends for coffee.

A study showed that city workers spend around £50 a week on coffee and snacks. That's up to £2,600 a year. But if you throw in newspapers, magazines and taxis that balloons out to around £112 per week - or £5,824 a year. Of course, if you include the cost of a weekly *quick drink* after work this can easily nudge closer to £10,000 a year, as Steven discovered.

But even if you eat at home, look at how money is wasted. Did you know that most Brits throw away 60% of fresh food such as bread, fruit, vegetables that they purchase each week from the supermarket? *That's 60p per every £1.*

Most people never identify how much they spend on the high margin end-of-aisle, treats included in their weekly shop. For example, chocolate, biscuits, soft drink, crisps etc.

OK, here are some small but important steps forward:

- From now on ask for receipts for *everything* you purchase. *Everything.*

- Buy 12 big freezer bags. (I buy those sturdy zip lock freezer bags). Label them January, February, March etc and then each month START putting *all* your receipts – month by month - inside the appropriately labelled bags.

- In addition, print out every monthly statement – bank, credit card, store card statements and put them in the bags as well.

- Read the statements carefully. Go line-by-line with a ruler and a red pen. A friend of mine discovered he was still being charged £35 per month for a gym membership he thought had cancelled two years earlier!

- Use Apps like *Spending Tracker, Yolt, Expensify, Quickbooks etc* to monitor your spending. Search your App store.

- You can use phone Apps like *Receipt Bank* to take a photo of the receipt and integrate them into *QuickBooks,* for example.

- Learn to use a spreadsheet and sort expenses into categories to see what you spend your money on and per category.

Most banks offer a free downloadable spreadsheet and there are hundreds of free online expense ledgers and Apps available that can be paired with your bank account.

In any case, you have to pay attention to what you spend your hard-earned money on.

Please do not ever say, "I don't want to do this because I am scared at what I might find." This is head-in-the-sand denial!

Get the information. You need to know your average expenses, and to do that you will need more than one month's expenses.

The group of young people who attended the money managing workshop collected *all* their expenses over 12 weeks. Once they got into the new habit of collecting receipts, printing out statements and checking, they quickly discovered what they wasted money on.

And they started to see spending patterns.

Importantly, look for surprises in your expenses. Look at your bank statements and receipts and the items your purchased and ask yourself how you ended up making that purchase. Was it on a whim or a impulse? For example, you popped out to buy bread and milk and came home with a new outfit!

Doing this activity will help you become aware of your spending behaviours and help you make better choices.

Lisa spent £400 a month - on average - on clothing.

She said, "How can that be? It's only £15 here and £25 there." But it all adds up! But note, her insight was that it was *per month* meaning it had become a habit.

By the way, *Skill #1 Monitoring* is very much connected to *Skill #2 Focusing*. Once you start monitoring your spending you can start setting clearer targets for reducing unnecessary expenses.

Lisa still likes buying new clothes but she has reduced that to around £100 per month. She used the other £300 per month she spent on clothes to pay off her credit card debt, *which now stays at zero.*

You should carefully review expenses like utilities, gas and electricity. You might discover you are paying too much. Or it could mean the way you use gas and electricity is expensive.

Did you know you can usually negotiate a better rate at any time?

A short phone call to your supplier will usually result in reduced bills. Most utility companies base your tariff on the number of rooms. We know *empty nesters* don't stay up late or run loads of appliances, don't use as much water or power or gas. They close off and turn off heating in unused rooms and therefore don't heat the whole house.

I was able to reduce my gas and electricity bill by 12% because I asked! And I also told them that the number of people in the dwelling had decreased. I saved £289 pa. That may not sound much as the saying goes, *Every little helps.*

The same principles apply at the business level.

A company had revenues of $1m and overheads of $900,000 per annum. That leaves $100,000 net profit.

They listed all overheads from most expensive down to the cheapest. They were able to negotiate 5% off their overheads. That's $45K! Their profit increased to £145K - nearly a 50% increase in profits.

Collect receipts, read statements, phone suppliers but get a much clearer picture of how you spend money each month.

Remember Steven? He dramatically reduced his entertainment costs. "First, I stopped buying rounds of drinks for mates. I now spend about £60 a week at the bar but I have cleared my credit card debt."

Smart money expert, Carl Richards, says people spend so

little time thinking about how they spend money. Reading bank statements and thinking about what you purchased and why is a great habit that will make you much better at managing your money.

Most wealth coaches suggest you allocate at least one hour a week to money managing activities such as reading statements and reviewing receipts and identifying the categories where you spend and waste money.

Recently I did a magazine quiz on *'What type of spender are you?'.* Nine questions reveal five types of spender - *Careful, Bargain Hunter, Self-Gifter, Retail Therapy-ist* and *Compulsive Shopper.*

You've probably guessed that I came out as a *Careful Spender.*

Quizzes can be fun but if it makes you more aware of your spending habits then they are invaluable.

As you will discover, awareness is the key to money mastery.

Your turn

- Do you know how much you spend each week, month, quarter, year? Using ideas in this chapter, what could you start doing to get a clearer picture of your spending?
- Review the six categories again on page 94 and see if you have a gut feel for where you spend the most money?
- Focus on discretionary spending. Where are you *obviously* wasting money? What do you need to STOP spending money on?

THE MONEY CHIMP

Money Activity #3: Saving

There is nothing better than the feeling of knowing you have surplus money set aside. Especially as savings.

The most cited basic wealth advice is: Save 10% of what you earn. If you are a wage earner, that means 10% of your *after-tax*, take-home pay. Let's say you earn £100 per week, after-tax. You save £10 a week. Over a year that's $520.

It doesn't sound much but some people have zero savings.

Josey has been saving 10% of everything she has earned since she was 14 years old. She had saved over £15,000. She has always had *enough* money in the bank and a sense of security.

Our drummer EARNS a lot but SPENDS more than he earns. And he saves NOTHING. And even after several years of being a highly paid session musician he has nothing - financially - to show for his efforts. He confronted that harsh reality in the money-managing workshop.

By contrast, a mate of mine was in a charting rock band and despite the temptation of a wild lifestyle, he lived modestly and channelled his earnings into savings and then property. When the band's fame faded he was the only band member with something to show for their success.

He still receives about $5,000 a year for music/performance

royalties but he says, "I'm so glad I put money away at the time and invested. I now own several properties that give me a comfortable post-rock star lifestyle."

Most movie, pop and sports stars shine for *about* four years, Very few have an enduring career. You may remember UK pop star, Shakin' Stevens from the 1970s? He knew that he wouldn't always be a charting pop star. I believe 40 years on, his property portfolio gives him a comfortable lifestyle simply because he saved money and invested wisely.

As a boy, Paul McCartney learned the value of saving and living within his means. And he understood property. He bought a property close to Abbey Road Studios, St John's Wood. If you walk past the house you can see the famous bathroom window that *she* came in through.

Apparently, Ringo Starr still owns the shops he bought in Chelsea in the mid 1960s'.

And I believe Mick Jagger's grand kids live in the properties he bought in Chelsea with earnings from his early days with the *Rolling Stones*. In those days Chelsea wasn't a prestigious suburb but reportedly, Jagger has done very nicely from property, and it appears he *can* get satisfaction. Despite his fame, it seems he never shook his accounting background! He definitely understood the value of managing money.

Michael Palin and Terry Gilliam of *Monty Python* fame are both on record for living well within their means. Even though at one point they were part of a famous comedy team they controlled their spending and invested well.

All these performers followed the pattern of making money at the height of fame and saving and investing for the future.

Even if you're not a pop star, save at least 10% of what you earn. When your funds reach a certain level, invest in something that pays a good rate of interest like an ISA or tax-free pension.

Trading mentor and entrepreneur, Jason Graystone agrees that you should first create a *liquidity cushion* of 3-6 months worth of living expenses in cash reserves. And he would agree to lock in the habit of saving 10% of your after-tax, take-home pay. But he would then encourage you to increase your savings goal by *1% per quarter*. So, in three months time you are saving 11%, then 12% and so on. Then, you would start to channel those savings into investments.

My son saved up enough money to invest in shares in his early 20s. Once you have a savings plan, don't touch it until you are ready to invest in shares, property or business.

An investment usually makes money faster than you could earn it over time.

As I discovered there is no point amassing savings and earning a piddling .001% in a bank account. A friend invested $10,000 in shares and over six years turned that into $40,000. Had he left that money in the bank it would have earned significantly less! He educated himself and sought good advice. You should too.

If you can't save 10%, save 5%. But regularly save *something* and don't ever spend it. Pretend that account doesn't exist.

Some people say they *can't* save. But that's not true. Everyone can save something. I have seen 18 year olds put £25 a week into an ISA. A year later they have been saving money in a tax-free environment that has earned good interest.

When we first moved from Australia to the UK in 2009, I saved £11,000 over two years. That money came from earnings, doing extra income projects and even selling off unwanted stuff like psychology books from my university days.

Troy sold a jet ski, a kayak, snow skis and diving gear that was gathering dust in his garage. That money cleared his credit card debt and paid off a huge chunk of his personal loan. As a result the loan period and repayments were significantly reduced.

OK, here's what works and what I recommend. It can be a tough call but its doable.

- Your savings plan starts with saving 10% of your after-tax, take-home pay. Don't *ever* touch it unless it is being channelled into a sound investment such as an ISA or property.
- Save at least £2,000 for unexpected bills and financial emergencies. You need an emergency fund.
- Start to save at least 3-6 months of average monthly living expenses to create a financial cushion. Most financial stress is the result of knowing that you have zero financial buffer or cash reserves. Cash reserves alleviate that stress and give you added protection and peace of mind.
- Start saving for future projects such as your education, or self development. Most established companies *invest* - and I do mean *invest,* not *spend* - at least 10% on self development.

Once you start to see results it encourages you to continue the savings habit.

Most money experts recommend *paying yourself first* by saving minimum, 10% of your take-home pay. They suggest never spending it unless you are investing it into something that is tax efficient and earns you a lot more than bank interest. (Seek advice from someone like a financial planner.)

Start by saving at least 10% and gradually increase it by 1% per quarter. Initially, it might not seem enough but it is still the best starting point for creating the savings habit.

I save 20% of everything I earn and apart from a small mortgage have no debts. I actually live well on less than 60% of my after-tax income. At my stage in life I do not have the money worries that plague many people my age.

And this can be true for you, too, once you get the savings habit.

Understand: you save to invest. Ultimately, you are aiming for financial independence.

But here's the problem: most people pay their bills, do their shopping, splash a little cash *and then* they try and save 10% from whatever is left over, which is usually 10% of very little … or nothing.

So, start by saving 10% of your after-tax income *first;* and then spend. But pay yourself first.

Again, good money managers save a set amount *before* they pay their bills, go shopping or splash some cash.

The five most important savings goals are:

- SAVE at least three to six months of living expenses.
- SAVE money for financial emergencies.
- SAVE at least 10% of your after-tax, take home pay; and increase that amount by 1% per quarter.
- SAVE for investment goals.
- SAVE for retirement.

Sounds good? Well, there's just one problem with being a good saver.

THE MONEY CHIMP

Warning: You Are Not An ATM Or An Interest-Free Bank

Here's a big heads up.

Trust me, once you get into the habit of saving you will become a magnet *for people who don't save* - usually family and friends. It seems that once you have money the letters *ATM* magically appear over your head like a huge neon sign.

Lisa is a good saver. But her brother isn't and he is always *borrowing* money from her. And he expects to borrow money from her because he's *family*. And in their family it's considered *selfish* to refuse to help someone who needs help.

Under those conditions, her saving plans repeatedly fell by the wayside.

Her brother cleaned her out of the £2,000 she had saved up to pay off a credit card bill. While he said he was *borrowing* the money, two years later she is yet to see any of that money repaid.

Worse, Lisa felt *guilty* for having money *and her brother knew how to make her feel guilty*. Saying *No* feels like a betrayal. Her brother Jason pouts and yells and gets angry. He just *has to* have the latest *X-Box*. And new trainers. He even begs and pleads her to help him pay his rent!

And Lisa feels responsible for Jason and ... lends him more money.

It took some convincing for her to realise that *she* was actually being *irresponsible* ... by continually bailing him out. She came to realise that she was, in fact, teaching Jason to depend on her by being responsible for his problems.

And let's just check that whole *you must help someone who needs help* rule. When Lisa talked to her parents a) they didn't realise Jason was leeching of his sister to the extent that he was; b) their rule is really about people *genuinely* less fortunate - not just lazy or indolent; and c) they thought Lisa was a fool for lending any money to Jason.

It pays to check. Lisa no longer lends money to Jason.

She has since, saved up for a deposit on a small bedsit apartment and three years later the value has increased enough for her to finance a larger apartment and rent the first!

That may not be your goal but for Lisa that has been a massive breakthrough in her relationship with money and the realisation of a dream!

So if you are a good saver, keep it quiet.

Get The Facts First

Any wealth coach will ask you to make a full list of what you spend money on and then *actively* look for ways to reduce your spending so you can start saving.

But that won't happen without the facts.

A London based programmer was ignoring the poor state of his finances and was even scared to do the ideas suggested in this book ... *in case it confirmed his worst fears!*

But after four months of getting the facts, he had a much clearer picture of his finances and made a very bold move. He found a better paid job, moved to Manchester where the rent was much cheaper and reduced his costs of living.

Three months later he had cleared his credit card debt. Then over a year had saved for a deposit on his own apartment.

"I knew I was being irresponsible with money but I was frightened to look. But once I got clear data on my finances I made better decisions and life started to improve, rapidly.

"Changing jobs *and* cities wasn't easy. I'll probably move back to London, eventually, but for now I'm saving money and getting ahead faster than I ever thought possible."

Here's a very smart tip. Most people get the idea about cutting back to save money. But they cut back on little things like coffees and lunches.

But you should definitely look at bigger expenses such as your energy bills. You might renegotiate your tariff and that can translate into significant savings.

They say, *Look after the pennies and the pounds will take care of themselves.* But you can be penny wise and pound foolish, too.

Ultimately, getting a clearer picture of how you spend your money will lead to better choices. And savings.

Your turn

- Are you good at saving money?
- Do you pay yourself first?
- Will you save at least 10% of your after-tax, take-home pay?
- Will you create a special savings account just for your 10% savings?
- Can you work out what three months worth of living expenses add up to?
- How much money are you going to save in an *emergency fund*?
- Do you need to create a Christmas fund?
- What's starting to make sense to you?
- Getting any ideas for action?

Money Activity #4: Investing

The number #1 advice given by all money experts is: *Spend less than you earn*. And this should allow you to save.

I've suggested you to save at least three to six months of living expenses, save for financial emergencies and use surplus cash to reduce debt. But the best reason for saving is to enable you to start investing.

Investing is the proven route to financial freedom because usually your investments increase in value much faster than your ability to earn the same amount of money over the same period of time.

Investing can involve borrowing money, and therefore going into debt, but it doesn't have to.

As mentioned, there is *good debt* and *bad debt*. *Good debt* is borrowing money to purchase something that *grows* in value such as a property. Bad debt is borrowing money for something that quickly *loses* value such as the latest smart phone.

Best-selling *Rich Dad, Poor Dad* author, Robert Kiyosaki suggests investing in tax deductible, income generating assets is the best form of *good debt*.

Your investments should provide you with an income, a dividend, growth or a healthy return if and when you sell. The four main investment strategies are *property, shares, cash* and *businesses*.

Residential Property

In the 1980s, I saved up $7,000 for a deposit and borrowed $11,000 and purchased a small residential property for $18,000.

I spent another $12,000 fixing it up and four years later sold that property for $65,000 with a profit of $54,000 (after paying for legal fees and stamp duty). I could never have saved $54,000 in four years!

I was a *20-something* with a young family and a first home buyer. And notice it was a *small* property and a *small* loan. It was not the biggest or the best. But that's how we got on the property ladder.

Plus I did most of the renovation work. To this day I know how to plaster, paint, fix electrics, tile, grout, replace glass, fix plumbing and a host of other handyman skills.

Now, I am not advising you to invest in property. But I do feel comfortable with residential property and it's always been good for me for two reasons.

Firstly, it seems every property has increased in value and therefore the equity acquired when sold.

Secondly, the increase in equity allowed me to buy a much nicer family home - with a reduced mortgage. But as I saved and paid down the debt, I was then able to release equity from the property and invest in rental property.

Property is an obvious investment choice for most people because you need somewhere to live. And it is usually better to be paying off the mortgage on your own home than renting than paying off someone else's mortgage.

Rental Property

If you have a mortgage and live in that home, your home is actually considered a *liability* because it *costs* you money.

However, if you *don't* live in it yourself and earn rental income it's deemed an *asset* because it *makes* you money.

Fred, a nurse with the *NHS* bought a small house in Bristol, but transferred to a hospital in Kent. Rather than sell his home, he decided to *rent out* his property in Bristol. The rental income not only pays his mortgage in Bristol but most of the rent on his flat in Kent, as well!

How clever is that?

Karen and Ian live and work in Reading but bought a small rental apartment in London which has already gone up in value. They are now intending to borrow against their London flat to buy *another* small flat.

Rental property is exciting because you are earning income from the property, your tenants are paying off your mortgage, you are getting the increase in value and you can borrow against the equity to buy more property.

Property investment specialists like Vicki Wusche or Steve Bolton teach investors how to achieve financial independence through investing in low cost, rental property.

Steve wrote *Successful Property Investing* and his company *Platinum Property Partners* offers specific training in *Houses of Multiple Occupation* (HMOs).

I mentioned Mick Jagger earlier. One of his first goals when *The Stones* started to make money was to buy a house and stop paying rent. At the time he bought low cost property in an *undesirable* suburb of London, called Chelsea!

Commercial Property

It doesn't have to be residential property. Malcolm bought a small industrial shed when he was 24 which turned into a lifetime love for commercial property. A bricklayer by trade, he specialises in building *off-the-plan* warehouses that earn him money before they are even built!

This section might sound like an advertisement for property, but property is just one investment strategy worth exploring.

Shares

Rob likes shares. He can't understand why anyone would lock their money up in bricks and mortar. He began share trading in university as a way of paying off his student loan. He developed a flair for doing the research needed to invest wisely in shares and over time, he has built an impressive portfolio in *penny* shares.

Cash

Ian is a financial planner who specialises in working with busy professionals who work hard and make a good income. Most of their money is tied up in a nice family home but they don't have spare *lifestyle cash*. Basically, they are asset rich and cash poor.

Ian's clients realise that turning 50 is a few short years away and they now realise they may not be able to fund their current lifestyle in their retirement, once they stop working.

Ian helps them to put their cash to better use than, say, a lease on an expensive European car. As I understand it, he unlocks equity in the family home and channels that money into high growth, tax-free environments like short-term ISAs and accessible pension schemes.

This investment strategy is worth exploring for *any one* at *any age,* but in any case, please seek qualified, licensed advice.

Businesses

I personally love business. My first service business cost me $500 to start and within a year I had turned that into a $32,000 profit. I love buying low and selling high and making money on the spread. I often encourage young people to start buying and reselling on *eBay*.

Don and Jeff teach people how to set up profitable *Fulfilled By Amazon (FBA)* businesses. They say a small investment in training and mentoring can turn into a high five or moderate six-figure business for the right person.

But which investment strategy is right for you?

Our 27-year old drummer said, "I'm focused on work, getting debt-free and saving money for a deposit on a flat." So, maybe property resonates most with him.

In any case, start by educating yourself. Read books and attend courses. The most successful investors invest time and money - *ongoing* - in education, training and professional advice. It is not a hit and miss, suck-it-and-see activity.

Right now, you might well be wasting your money with little to show for your efforts. But a year goes by very fast. And five years even faster. One day, you might realise you should have started learning about and investing a lot sooner.

Your turn

- Of the four main investment vehicles (property, shares, cash, businesses) which one sounds about right to you? Why?
- Pick one and do a web search, visit a library or go online to your bank and do some background reading.
- Are you starting to see the link between earning, saving and investing? What's going through your mind?
- Start playing money games like *Monopoly, Life* or *Cashflow*.

Habit #5: Giving

It is good to give. But hang on, what's happening here? I just urged you to focus on saving and reducing your spending, and now I'm saying give some of it away?

That's exactly what I am saying.

We know that people who have their finances under control are generally more charitable. *Giving* means giving money to others with no expectation or requirement to be repaid.

Most people give money to charities or causes. Some people give money to a church. And most of us give money to family or friends as gifts. Not loans.

Giving works. It's actually good for you to give. We are hard wired to contribute and we feel bad when we can't help; *or can help, but don't*. Giving helps someone who is *genuinely* less fortunate than yourself; usually living under adverse conditions unlikely to change for the better, anytime soon.

But give wisely.

I used to give money to the homeless on the street but after volunteering with *Crisis at Christmas* I learned that the money is much better *donated* to a reputable charity like *Crisis*, *Red Cross* or *Unicef* who know how to put your donations to good use.

Crisis don't recommend giving money directly to the homeless or to beggars because rarely is it put to good use. As we now know, a lot of beggars are in fact, working for rackets. For a while, in London, everywhere you went there were women from Eastern Europe begging with baby or a small child. Sadly, most of these beggars are the face of organised crime.

There is a woman that works the overground trains from Stratford in London. She limps the length and breadth of the train begging. Her limp suggests a profound disability. Get off the train and follow her and away from the station, you'll discover she walks just fine. We all have to make a living and feed families I suppose. But it is deceptive and makes fools of good people who give from compassion.

Crisis taught me: only give money to registered and reputable charities.

Yes, charities have operating costs but don't let that stop you from donating. Do your homework and find a charity you feel comfortable with because giving is good for others and giving fuels your drive for success.

Wealth coach, Sarano Kelley recommends donating 10% of your income to charities. I know a woman that attended a high profile church and they convinced her to give 10% of her salary as a tithe. Not 10% of her *after-tax*, take home pay, but 10% of her *pretax pay*. Avoiding feeling like a sinner, put her under considerable emotional pressure and practical hardship.

But is still good to give something. If you can't give money start by donating your *time*.

For many years, I volunteered at the annual *Crisis at Christmas* programme in London and have learnt a lot about my own values and life goals by volunteering.

Make a commitment now to choose a charity that you feel comfortable with; and then help out. Being a volunteer offers a range of life affirming benefits for the charity, for you and their beneficiaries.

What About Giving To Family And Friends?

I enjoy *giving* money to my children and I give money to family and friends on special occasions such as birthdays. You might too. But avoid giving money to family or friends if it's to supplement their income, especially if they somehow make you feel guilty for saying *No*. It is a bad habit to start.

If someone asks to *borrow* money, they are inferring they intend to *pay it back*. If they don't pay you back they are taking advantage of your good nature. They are treating you like an interest-free bank, and worse, if you are a soft touch, you are training them to be irresponsible.

If they ask you to *give* them money that's different. Giving is not *lending* money. And lending money is not a *gift*. Giving is okay, but giving should never hurt the giver.

Remember Lisa? Her brother Jason borrowed £2,000 from her and is yet to repay any of that money. He rationalises that somehow she is obligated to help him because he is family.

Her mother says, "If you were stupid enough to give him money, then you are a fool." She gets no thanks or recognition for her generosity.

Lisa should have clearly established *'This is a loan that has to be repaid by <date>'.* That is the *only* reason I will *lend* you money. That's how banks work. Try asking your bank for a gift. It's *not* a gift. It's a loan.

Think about it this way. If her brother went to a bank what would they say? They would want collateral. In other words, what have you got worth £2,000 ... *plus the fees,* to set up the loan and administer it, *plus bank charges, plus interest* if you miss the payments *plus penalties* if you default on the loan?

Lisa's brother is treating her like an unconditional, interest-free bank. But it's worse, because he has zero intention of paying back what he supposedly *borrowed*.

And incredibly, he feels *entitled* to his sister's money!

Worse, every time Lisa *lends* him money she is teaching him to be irresponsible. His thinking goes something like, "If I get into trouble, Lisa has cash."

But what else could she have done?

She could have said, "This is a *gift*. You do not have to repay any of it."

The problem is she needs the money herself and can't afford to give it anyway. And she wants Jason to repay the money. So, be clear, it's *not* a gift.

She knows from long experience that whenever she *lends* money to her brother, he will never repay the money that she has worked hard to earn, and something he is more than capable of doing himself.

Ironically, he resents the fact that Lisa *has* money to lend. A sense of entitlement will do that to you.

This is such a tough issue in a close-knit family where one person applies guilt-provoking and emotional pressure to get a *free ride*. You have to resist the urge to be *nice*, helpful or a rescuer. (This dynamic is covered in detail in the book *The Energy of Money*.)

In my own extended family, there was a relative who spent all his parent's inheritance money, and then tried to *borrow* his sister's inheritance as well! And he got angry when she refused. Family members will accuse you of being unfair but they are usually covering up issues they don't want to face, such as, they are being lazy or irresponsible.

And they *do* want a free ride. *Google* the *Free Rider Effect*. It is very well documented that the *free rider effect* can quickly lead to more serious problems.

I am a business coach and one of my clients, Peter, runs a successful agricultural irrigation supply company. Peter asked me to coach one of his young managers, Brian, who managed one of the stores located in a remote country region.

Brian seemed pleasant enough but I quickly sensed something was wrong. He kept missing coaching appointments, cut sessions short and rarely did any of the activities we agreed on. And there were other things that didn't add up.

I confronted Brian. I said he was wasting Peter's training budget. And I said I would recommend that Peter take a much closer look at Brian, the operation, the staff ... *and the accounts*.

Brian then confessed that he had racked up gambling debts and that he was stealing money from the company through pricing scams. Apparently, he would inflate the price of products, pocket a cash deposit and put the sale through the business at the correct cost, with Peter none the wiser.

At this point, Peter said he would sack him and have him charged by the police. Brian pleaded and begged for a reprieve. He said he had two children to support and if he lost his job he'd lose his marriage, his kids and his house. Peter still fired him but took pity and *dropped the charges.*

Gradually, Peter discovered the full extent of Brian's scam. He had siphoned off over $235,000. Some months later, we heard he had done the *same* thing to his next employer, only this time he was charged and jailed for three years.

Why have I included this story? Because Jason reminds me of Brian. Brian believed he was *entitled* to that money and was contemptuous of Peter's success.

Brian rationalised that Peter wouldn't miss it and didn't feel any remorse or responsibility for his actions. And he even blamed Peter for putting temptation in his way!

Peter and Lisa, both kind and compassionate people, had their heartstrings tugged and both went against their better judgment.

But people like Brian are only grateful for a short time and soon go back to their old habits. And they do not actually appreciate or value the compassion or generosity of others, anyway.

The moral here is: *Giving should not hurt the giver.*

We sponsored a child in Ethiopia for many years. This little girl will never be able to repay what we have invested into her future. However, our sense of fulfillment has been immense.

A business colleague, Jeff, sponsors over 1,500 kids through his business. One of those kids grew up and eventually went to university and emerged with a political law degree and is now a major policy maker in Uganda. That young man has grown into a mature adult who is making a positive difference in his country.

That would not have been possible without Jeff's sponsorship.

So the tips here are:

- It's good to give to others who are less fortunate.
- Giving shouldn't hurt the giver.
- It is not good to lend money to people who are more than capable of helping themselves.
- If it's a *loan* then you should be clear that the loan be repaid.

Finally, *give* thanks. We all have so much to be grateful for starting with the love and support of people in our lives. Be thankful that you *can* create the life you want. There actually *is* an abundance of opportunity if you just look.

Gratitude is a huge element of giving.

Ultimately, aim to give back.

Your turn

- What do you feel about donating money to charities?
- Of all the charities you know which one appeals the most to you? Why that charity?
- Do a web search about the charity that interests you most?
- Make a list of people you lend money to? What have you learned about the people who borrow money from you? Especially, what have you learned about people who don't repay their *loans*?
- This week find a charity and donate £5. Notice how that feels.
- Cultivate an attitude of gratitude. What can you be grateful for today?

THE MONEY CHIMP

Part 4

The Five Money Managing Skills

THE MONEY CHIMP

Money Skill #1 Monitoring

For the next 30 days monitor your expenses. Write down *every* financial transaction. If you spend £1.50 on hot chips, write it down. If you spend £15 on a book, write it down. If you buy a $2 lottery ticket, write it down. If you spend $2.35 at the grocer on the way home, make a note of that as well. Track everything you spend for the next 30 days.

Ideally, get receipts for everything.

You cannot and will not work out what money you need until you know how much money you spend each month, down to the last penny.

Good money managers know how much they spend.

Here's a fact: wealthy people monitor their money; poor people don't. That's one reason why poor people stay poor. You need to identify *exactly* how much you spend; and what you spend it on. That data will help you set realistic targets and show you where you need to reduce your spending.

Monitoring uses the skills of recording and analysing your spending using the skills of *collating, data entry* and *reconciling*.

- **Collating** means collecting all receipts, bills and statements as mentioned. But it also means sorting that information into expense categories.

- **Data entry** means entering that information into a notebook, spreadsheet or ledger. Essentially you are showing money in and money out and by category (gas, rent, food shopping, school fees, train travel etc).

- **Reconciling** means cross checking the ledger against the actual bank statements and receipts so that everything matches and tallies and balances!

Once you start monitoring you might be shocked at what you discover. Most people will find their bank statements include bank interest, fees and charges automatically deducted from their account.

It stunned me to discover I was paying about $48 a month in late fees and interest charges on my credit card. That's nearly $500 a year! If you are not good at managing your money now, I guarantee this is happening!

But the good news is monitoring starts to pay off quickly.

I discovered I was still paying £35 a month for an old gym membership that I thought I had cancelled.

And I discovered I was still paying £5 per month for a online business membership I don't use. £60 a year isn't a lot but it's £60 I don't need to be spending.

Remember the girl who spent £400 a month on clothing? She didn't know it was that much until she started monitoring her spending.

Monitoring helps you realise how much you are spending and gives you choices.

Kevin was paying £1,836 PCM for a flat that wasn't that great. He found another flat that was smaller but of a better standard for £1,100 PCM. That's a saving of over £736 PCM or £8,832 a year.

Ian noticed the direct debit for energy bills increasing.

So, he renegotiated his gas and electricity and saved £36 per month. That's over £432 a year.

When Ian checked his receipts he estimated he was spending nearly £10,000 a year on alcohol and nearly £3,224 on cigarettes. Combined, that's almost a 10% deposit on a small flat!

Lisa checked her mobile phone bills and usage. By changing her mobile phone plan and ditching streaming services she saved $32 a month. Ben's phone bills showed he was averaging £80 a month on downloads. That's £960 a year. He also jettisoned his internet plan and changed his phone habits. His phone bill now is a minuscule £13.70 a month.

Our drummer was shocked when he worked out how much extra debt he was incurring on his credit and store cards in late fees. "Doing the maths really motivated me to clear that debt! It was tough at first but I now manage my credit card – it doesn't manage me!"

You can't get savings like these without monitoring.

Here's how I monitored my expenses for many years.

Start by getting 12 freezer bags and label them - January, February, March etc - one for each month of the year.

Start by putting any income statements or pay slips in the bag.

Then put your monthly savings and credit card bank statements in the appropriate month-labelled bag.

Then the bills. Identify any amount that's set up as a direct debit or standing order to be automatically deducted from your bank account by a supplier such as gas, rent and council rates.

Then start collecting receipts for everything. Train tickets, fuel, meals, food shopping. Everything.

If you draw money out of an ATM put that receipt in the bag, too. If you can't get a receipt write the purchase down on a scrap of paper and put that note in the bag. To make reconciling easier collate the receipts in date order.

If you make a small petty cash purchase, include that. For example, I bought a *Snickers* bar for a $1 at a petrol station. I wrote down the amount and the date on a piece of note paper and threw that in the bag.

At the end of the month get all your bank statements and all your receipts. Get a ruler and a highlighter and go down the list and match as many receipts as you can to the statements. You're trying to identify your total income and expenditure for each month.

Then you're going to sort out what you spend your money on into the categories I listed earlier - liabilities, recurring bills, periodic bills, consumer debt, living expenses and discretionary spending.

Years ago, I did this manually in an exercise book with ruled columns. Nowadays, I use a spreadsheet that shows amounts in columns labelled *date, description, amount, total* and *sub-totals per category* such as phone, rent, transport, meals, bank fees, postage, stationery, medical, insurances, pets, loans etc.

Date	Details	Cheque Number / Payment Type	Total Amount	Materials	Phone	Travel (Rail / Fuel)	Subsiste Meals
16/10/2019	Biz Meals	CC	4.75				
16/10/2019	Train	CC	24.8			24.8	
16/10/2019	Parking	CC	4.7			4.7	
16/10/2019	Lulu	CC	20			20	
17/10/2019	DVLA	CC	21.5			21.5	
17/10/2019	Webbs	CC	2.95				
17/10/2019	Webbs	CC	29.44				

As an example, I know exactly how much I spend on train fares, parking, stationery or food shopping every month; and how much I spent on average each month per year.

Interestingly, if you talk to a financial planner or a wealth coach they will want this detailed information.

OK, time to stop right here!

Some of you will have already glazed over, some may have lost the will to live! And you are probably thinking, *OCD alert!* I hate to say it but, yes, you need to be a little obsessive about this at first. You need to know your numbers.

Remember Emily? It was her husband Patrick who asked her to get receipts for everything and tally them up at the end of the month. She felt he was prying *and* judging her. And she hated Patrick asking, "Did you get a receipt for lunch today?"

But she started collecting receipts. It became a habit. And then she saw that she was spending around £1,200 on lunches each month!

In my case, I was able to reduce my electricity bill by about £289 by monitoring expenditure and then asking for a better rate. It doesn't sound much, I know, but combined with other savings it adds up. But I'd much rather spend that £289 on birthday or Christmas presents.

My brother, Pip, was able to reduce his energy bills by around £300 a year simply by asking for a better tariff.

You'll discover that once you start monitoring, you want to track more! Melanie got into the swing of monitoring. She went through every credit card bill with a fine tooth comb and quickly realised that the bulk of her £9,000 debt was on beauty treatments, clothes, shoes, accessories and dining out.

Young people tell me *It's too hard* but once they do start monitoring they all say, *I wish I'd done this a lot sooner.*

Monitoring lets you analyse your spending, but it also allows you to forecast your future spending. Then start budgeting.

You might also rethink expensive habits. Steven no longer spends £180 a weekend on alcohol any more and Melanie now spends less than £100 a month on clothes now. Without monitoring you just keep wasting money.

Your turn

- Print out all your bank statements (deposit, loans, credit cards, store cards) and read them.

- Highlight any standing orders. Highlight all fees and charges. Importantly, check that you are not still paying for things you no longer use such as gym memberships.

- List every bill you receive and compile a list all your current suppliers like electricity, gas, rates, rent, insurance etc. You may need to do this over three–six months because some bills only appear quarterly or annually such as MOT or TV license.

- Get 12 plastic freezer bags and label them for each month of the year.

- Start collecting receipts for everything you buy and put them into those bags.

- At the end of the month look at all the receipts you've collected. What are you noticing? Any insights about what you spend money on?

- Set up *mobile phone budget alerts* from your bank to monitor your spending.

- Last question: how is this book landing? Are you getting benefit? Is it making sense? Importantly, what have you decided to do as a result of what you've read so far?

Money Skill #2 Focusing

If monitoring is all about clearly identifying how you spend your money, then focusing is all about identifying goals, targets and priorities.

You might want to reduce your credit card debt from £973 to zero. Or you might want to save up £1,400 for an overseas holiday. Or you might simply want to carry £100 in your wallet to spend on movie tickets or dining out.

To improve your ability to manage money you need to have specific goals and priorities - *and focus on them*.

To set clear goals you need accurate information about your income and expenditure gathered in the monitoring stage. As you can see monitoring and focusing work together.

As far as money is concerned there are three targets to focus on:

- Targets to *increase* something (earn more)
- Targets to *decrease* something (spend less)
- Targets to *maintain* something (save more)

In each case, your goals should be specific. You might set the target of saving £1,000 over the next 12 months to pay for next Christmas so that you don't spend the next six months paying off a credit card debt.

Aside from a mortgage, Christmas credit card debt is the most common debt burden for many families.

If you have monitored well, you now have clear targets. Having clear targets helps you make better decisions regarding what to do with your money.

Our drummer set the target of reducing his credit card debt from £7,000 to zero.

Remember the couple who racked up £41,000 in credit card debt? Well, before they could reduce that debt they needed to know their income and their expenditure – *exactly*. Despite being dual income, highly paid professionals they discovered they were in a real mess. On average, they paid back £1,900 per month over the next two years.

Actually, they played the *10% Debt Reduction Game*. Their first payment was £4,100; 10% of £41,000. That took the bill down to £36,900. Their next payment was £3,690 and so on. By month 22, the debt was down to £4,041 and they paid it off entirely. It was of course a little more with bank interest and charges, but you get the idea.

Their goal involved living frugally for two years. They sold unwanted items, they took extra jobs, they stopped buying items they didn't need, they moved to cheaper accommodation. They took a *whatever it takes* approach. And they worked closely with the bank to whittle that figure back to zero. Not everyone is that driven. *But it shows you that it can be done.*

Author of *The Money Tree*, Diana Mathew was driving home from work and blacked out at the wheel of her new car. The accident left her with hefty repair bills, but she then discovered the car was uninsured!

She negotiated with the finance company to repay that debt but then a recession hit. She lost her job.

That lead to missed mortgage repayments and the bank moved to foreclose. By this stage she was $8,000 in debt and barely making ends meet with no possible way she of catching up in the foreseeable future.

The first thing she did was list her debts and set a realistic time frame to clear them. Then she divided her after-tax income into three groups. 10% went into a savings account; 20% was used to pay bills and reduce debts; and she learned to live on the remaining 70%.

She listed *all* her liabilities and expenses. *Every* bill was scrutinised. She phoned every supplier and explained the situation and wherever possible a better rate was negotiated. Ironically, everyone was helpful. No one wanted to see her go under.

She got receipts for *everything* and analysed her spending patterns. She eliminated wasteful spending in her weekly shop - soft drinks, crisps, biscuits, cakes.

And she stopped buying coffees and take-aways. She would say, 'Let's *not* do lunch, coffee or drinks.' She took a packed lunch to work.

She cancelled the gym membership, the dance classes, the tennis lessons. Standing orders for clubs and charities all got cancelled, too. Understand, she was between a rock and a hard place. Anything wasteful had to go.

She reduced or eliminated any superfluous loans. And she ditched most of her insurances.

She also went on a financial witch-hunt for hidden fees and charges. She paid her credit card on time.

She got a new job and worked extra hours, and, worked small part-time jobs.

She set aside money for emergencies; and saved 4% of her income, then 5%, then 6%, then finally, 10% of her income

She started reading everything she could on debt reduction and went to free courses that developed her personal finance skills and her relationship with money. And four months later she was 100% debt free and had $2,000 in savings.

She then wrote a book called *The Money Tree* explaining how she did it. *The Money Tree* was a hit and made her one of the best-selling personal finance authors in Australia and her simple *get-out-of-debt* system has since helped families worldwide.

At the heart of the book is the skill of monitoring. She could not have gotten this result without the facts. Monitoring and focusing enabled her to make some very smart choices with one goal: *to be debt-free as fast as possible*.

Getting out of debt must become a much higher priority than buying a new handbag, owning the latest *smart* gadget, smoking or shouting your mates to an expensive round of drinks every Friday night.

Once out of debt you can set targets for improving your life like taking a well-earned holiday or owning your own home. You might set a goal of saving £300 per month for the next 25 years and retiring a millionaire!

Setting priority goals works closely with the skill of monitoring.

As mentioned, performance falls into three categories.

You must focus on:

- Things you need to **STOP** doing.
- Things you need to **START** doing.
- And things you need to **CONTINUE** doing (because its working).

Focusing is important because you identify specific things that need to change. Focusing allows you to decide where your money is better spent. For example, spending money on alcohol could be much better spent on reducing a credit card debt.

- **STOP** – stop spending so much on things that waste money such as cigarettes, alcohol, dining out, shoes, clothing, gaming, gambling.
- **START** – start doing things like reducing your credit card debts, saving for a holiday, or Christmas and birthdays, repaying a student loan faster.
- **CONTINUE** - continue with your savings plan.

Focusing requires accurate information. That means you need to carefully monitor, track and analyse what you earn and spend. Only then can you make informed choices.

There is no point setting a savings goal if you don't know where you currently waste money.

Remember the guy who moved from a flat of £1,836 a month to a flat for £1,100? Reducing expenditure to save money had to become a priority. To do that he had to move out of the city. The train fare went up by £200 per month but that was still £500 cheaper than where he was living previously. By the way, expenses like rates and utilities dropped accordingly.

It sounds simple but it isn't easy which is why most people don't get the results they need. It takes clear thinking and discipline. Determination and persistence. It most likely will involve some tough choices. But focus anyway.

Consider: what do you want more? What is of a higher priority?

I would love the latest model computer and a new car, but my data says, it's not time for either. Financing a new car will create more financial stress, right now.

Just so you know, wealth coach, Ann Wilson, says you should have dreams and set goals that are bigger than paying the rent.

Sarano Kelley in *The Game* says setting clear goals and targets will transform your relationship with money. Setting goals is about deciding what kind of life you want to live. And what sort of lifestyle you want?

So, what sort of lifestyle do you want? You have to imagine it in detail.

My friend Jake makes a very good point. "When my wife and I first got married we did not have a lot of money. We used to play *Let's pretend*. We would walk down the beach and imagine the sort of home we wanted to live in. The sort of car we wanted. The holidays we would go on. Things like that. It was a lot of fun. And most of those dreams came true."

This book is about taking small steps in the right direction. There is solid research that says having clear targets leads to long-term success. Life always improves once you are clear on the direction you are headed. And you take action.

Your Turn

- You've read this far – what are some obvious financial goals (or targets)?
- What have you already identified as *needs attention* or *needs sorting*?
- What's an obvious financial target you'd like to work on within the next 90 days?
- If you have racked up credit card debt what plan cou d you come up with to reduce or eliminate that debt within the next 90 days?

THE MONEY CHIMP

Money Skill #3 Reducing Your Spending

You've probably worked it out, by now. *Monitoring, focusing* and *reducing* go together.

Reducing is the skill you need to acquire in order to save more, reduce debts and live on less than you earn. The first goal might be to learn to live on less than 70% of your take-home, after-tax pay.

Just about every wealth book says save 10% of your take-home, after-tax pay; use 20% to reduce your debts; and learn to live on the remaining 70% of your income.

If I make a $1 after-tax, 10c gets saved, 20c goes towards reducing debts and I live on 70c. Apply that strategy to your current weekly salary and watch what happens.

There are several debt reduction strategies that work such as accelerated debt payments and debt eliminator programmes that get you to list all your debts and repayments and eliminate the smallest debts first.

But these strategies don't work unless you cut spending.

Use the information you gathered in the *Monitoring* stage along with the goals you identified in the *Focusing* stage to cut spending in the *Reducing* stage.

Do you now understand just how it is so easy to spend more than you earn? Most people spend 130% of their weekly income. This means they live beyond their means that results in chronic money worries.

Reducing is the skill of cutting back your spending. You will not manage your money effectively unless and until you learn to cut your spending.

This doesn't mean becoming excessively frugal or tight. I am talking about reducing spending on things that you already know are a complete waste of your money such as exceeding your mobile phone plan in order to stream games or movies.

In the last chapter, I gave two examples of people that went to extreme measures to get out of debt. Most people don't have that level of resolve or discipline to go even one week let alone 22 months.

But they did not go it alone. They sought help and support from suppliers, banks, customers, bosses, and of course, family and friends.

Reducing and monitoring go hand-in-hand. You need the data. There is no way around it. You need to know *exactly* what's happening with your spending, so you know where to trim.

Whenever I talk about *reducing*, people imagine they will sacrifice their lifestyle. Honestly, if you are in debt you don't have the lifestyle you imagine you have.

The guy that *borrows* from his sister knows deep down that his lifestyle is being funding by someone else's efforts. There is no accountability there. And he resents the fact he needs his sister's help! That isn't even remotely an enviable lifestyle.

These ten principles are a reality check. If you don't decided to get some ownership over managing your money, ultimately, you are wasting your time reading this book.

Reducing means changing your habits.

Remember how Diana Mathew said, "Let's *not* do lunch"? How Steven said, *No* to his drinking buddies and Melanie said *No* to clothes shopping? Who or what do you need to say *No* to?

This might mean saying *No* to lending money to family and friends. Be clear if your family or friends borrowed money from a bank they would be charged the principle and the interest.

Rarely do family and friends repay money they have *borrowed*. So, stop *lending* money. You are not a bank, an ATM machine or a registered charity.

Remember the old saying: *Giving is good as long as it doesn't hurt the giver.*

Reducing requires you to clearly identify where you need to cut back. Start with whatever seems obvious to you right now like socialising, clothes shopping, doing lunch. You may also need to trim some not-so-obvious habits like cancelling a dis-used gym membership.

Get the information. It might take a short time to get a clear picture because some expenses only occur on a periodic basis. But this is why you collect receipts and read bank statements.

Once Emily started collecting receipts and adding them up she discovered she was spending £1,200 a month on social meals. It became a lot easier to say *No* once she realised saying *Yes* was so expensive. Diana Mathew simple cancelled all dining out and social spending.

I was concerned about the high cost of our energy bills. My energy provider installed new meters along with a device that shows real-time energy consumption. I became a lot more conscious of energy use because I now have the information.

One couple significantly reduced their winter energy bills through installing roofing insulation, by closing doors and by turning off the radiators in unused rooms.

Cost reduction expert, Nigel Ward wrote a practical book called *Using Less Stuff!* (see *Amazon*) to help *business owners* save money on everything from utilities to energy consumption. But Nigel says these principles are easily applied to *householders*.

"Turn your central heating down one or two degrees. You will be just as comfortable at 18 as you are at 20 but your energy bills will be significantly less."

"Switch to LED light globes. Air your laundry rather than using the tumble drier. Wash your dishes by hand instead of using the dishwasher. Monitor the use of anything that draws power."

"Importantly, switch suppliers if you have to. Anyone can and should renegotiate a better tariff. Why would you want to give good money away to a energy company, for goodness sakes!"

"These are simple things *even you* can do to cut costs."

Nigel says to ask for a regular review of your bills especially if you pay via direct debit.

Last year, we had a warm Spring and a long Summer so while we weren't using the heating our energy provider was still deducting the same rate that was then held in credit. So check if you are eligible for a refund. That's money that should be in your bank, not theirs! My refund paid for about half of Christmas last year.

I gave an example earlier of a company that shaved 5% off their overheads and saved over £45,000. You can do that, too.

If you own a car you are most likely wasting money by speeding. David Wilson is a fuel consultant who helps his clients achieve average fuel savings of 14% by simply training drivers to slow down as they approach and then leave intersections and traffic lights. His clients typically spend £22m pa on fuel, so a 14% saving of £3.08m is significant. That's the cost of several new lorries.

But he says those two simple driving habits will cut vehicle costs for *any* motorist. His message is: *Slow down and save*. The knock-on benefit includes reduced service and maintenance fees.

Wealth Chef, Ann Wilson says, "Controlling your finances is about transforming your future."

The trick to transforming your finances is accurate data.

Your Turn

- Where do you obviously need to cut spending in the next 90 days?
- What needs eliminating all together?
- Get a list of all your bills and check if any of those could be renegotiated. As an exercise call one of your suppliers and tell them you'd like to find ways to reduce your energy bill. Check if they can offer you a better rate or tariff?
- What things do you buy right now that *you know* you actually don't need?
- Make sure you get receipts for everything and read your bank statements.

Money Skill #4 Developing Your Financial Smarts

I hope by now you are forming the picture that reversing your money woes and taking charge requires information. But it also requires you understand the information. That requires to invest in your own financial education and develop your skills by applying what you are learning.

You will never wake up one morning knowing how to save money or invest in an ISA, real estate or shares unless you improve your financial literacy and start honing your skills.

People who are good with their money search the internet, read books and magazine articles, attend short courses and seek advice. So, set aside time to educate yourself about how money works.

Steve Bolton runs a UK-based company called *Platinum Property Partners* that teaches people how to build wealth and achieve financial freedom through investing in property.

Steve says, "Ongoing personal and professional development will make the biggest difference to the level of success and financial freedom you achieve. Don't make the mistake of *not* investing time and money in your personal and professional development. Without a doubt it starts with learning how to manage your money."

Whatever you can do to improve your knowledge of finance, do it. Even if that starts with reading books on saving money.

An obvious place to start is in your local library; in the *Finance* section. Start with any books on *Saving Money* or *Debt Reduction*. At the end of the book I've included a list of some good money managing books I found located at my local library.

Most books will cover aspects of earning, spending, saving, investing and giving. And other books will cover monitoring, targeting, reducing, developing skills and taking action.

Just make sure the books you choose are current.

Have you ever been into a library and see old software guides? You are not going to borrow a book on *Excel 2000*, right? No, because its way it's out of date. It's the same with money books. Check the publication date.

Sure, some books offer timeless advice. I read a book on how to save money on weekly shopping that was written in 1934 during the Depression that is as relevant today as it was then. It reported: *We throw away 60% of purchased fresh produce.* That has not changed in almost 90 years.

Of course, I'm not suggesting you eat stale food. Rather, work out the right quantities of fresh produce that you need for a week and purchase accordingly.

I would encourage you to read Adam Smith's *The Wealth of Nations*. But be warned, initially, this is a hard read because it is over 200 years old. But I am amazed at how relevant this book is to anyone who wants to understand money; and wealth.

Written in 1776, this book has shaped and dominated the economics of the world since, and once you get into it, you will find it hard to put down. You can download Smith's book as a PDF, for free.

But let's go with something more current.

A great place to find money management advice and training is on your bank's website. Most banks offer free information, tips, tutorials and tools on managing money. And a range of online and downloadable tools like spreadsheets, and budgeting Apps.

Most people have no idea how much good information and personal advice is offered by their bank, for free. The big secret is to do a little bit every day.

Bank staff can also refer you to qualified experts who can help you with budgeting, planning, savings, loans, insurance and so on. Start by logging on to your bank's website or visit your nearest branch.

Steve Bolton strongly emphasises the benefits of getting professional advice as well as coaching and mentoring.

Your accountant offers a lot more than simply filing your *tax return* each year. They can offer practical advice and support such as bookkeeping, tax advice, budgeting and forecasting.

Financial advisors can help build a personal action plan suited to your needs and goals. And they can provide ongoing support. Ken and Peter are two experienced financial advisors based in Wales who specialise in ensuring their clients plan and fund their future - sooner.

"A lot of young people are leaving university and earning good starting salaries. One of our clients is a 24 year old programmer who earns £140,000 a year! He has been smart enough to seek investment advice now. Most young people will simply spend their money and end up with little to show for their efforts."

No one can help you if you don't know what money you earn, spend or save; or if you have no goals or plans.

Wealth coach, Simon Jeffries also advises younger clients earning good salaries.

"Here's what works. The ones who get ahead think about their future and start *planning* sooner. And it's amazing how quickly you can get ahead financially with the right plan."

He observes that those who struggle and end up with little to show for their efforts, usually can't be bothered planning. And they don't invest in knowledge and skills.

"Most people are reluctant to borrow a *free* book from a library let alone pay for a training course or work with a mentor that can help them become debt-free, financially-free or even wealthy, sooner."

Think what it would mean to be wealthy. Think about all the benefits of being in charge of your money. Then think about all the negative consequences of *not* changing your habits, beliefs, learning new skills or changing your behaviour.

You can be debt-free within the next three to six months if you make it a priority. But you'll need to change some beliefs, learn new ways of thinking and apply new money managing skills.

The key is to start with the obvious. If the most obvious thing is to reduce your credit card bills, search the web for tips on reducing credit card bills.

The best advice is to start reading. Old or new books, start reading. You will find a lot of information repeats, sure, and there is also conflicting advice, but keep reading, anyway.

I read over 143 books in order to write *The Money Chimp* and most of the best money managing advice was identified in about the first 12 books. But I still kept reading, picking up good ideas, here and there.

Reading helps but in the end it must result in action. You must clearly identify how much money you earn, how much you spend and what you spend your money on each month and each year.

You need that information to help you decide what action is required.

Take The Money Managing Skills Quiz

One of the best ways to invest in yourself is to take the online *Money Chimp* quiz to identify your current level of money managing skills. People who do *The Money Chimp* quiz say it was incredibly helpful in pinpointing strengths and weaknesses.

You answer 35 money questions and you get back a detailed 20-page PDF report. The report gives you clear feedback and suggestions on each of the money managing habits *Earn, Spend, Save, Invest, Give*; and skills *Monitor, Focus, Reduce, Develop* and *Action*.

The illustration below is a sample of the full report.

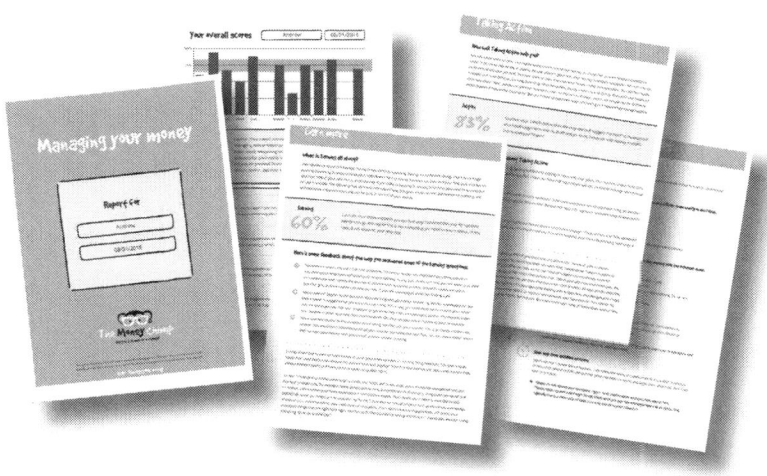

You also get a graph of your individual results, and an overall score, like the one below. Take a moment to review this graph. This person needs a lot of across-the-board help. Let me explain.

Your overall scores

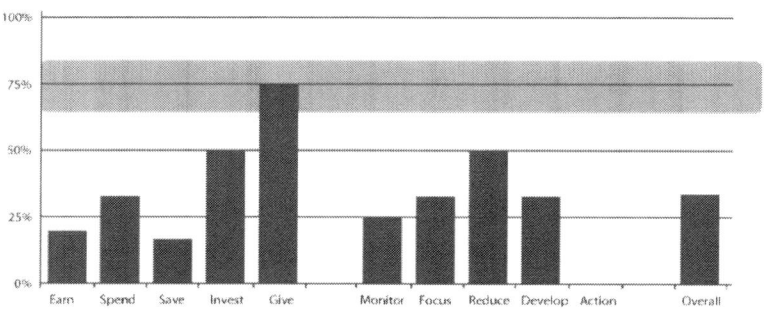

On the left hand side you can see a scale ranging 0-100%; a horizontal grey zone set at the 75% mark; and some vertical bars ranging in different heights.

Ideally, those vertical bars need to be somewhere *inside* that grey zone. If they are *outside* the horizontal grey zone - *too high or too low* - it means it's an area requiring your attention.

This graph suggests this person doesn't earn enough, they spend too much, and don't save. But they are good giver.

They also need to pick up skills in monitoring their finances, they need to set targets and focus, and improve their financial literacy skills. It appears this person may already be working on reducing their spending because it is trending towards being in range.

In addition to the graph, you also get detailed feedback on how you answered *every question with suggestions for improvement*.

Essentially, you get a personalised report on your current money-managing skills.

People who do *The Money Chimp* quiz say:

- "This was really useful, practical information."
- "I knew a lot of this already but it was scary - and also good - to see what I knew, confirmed in black and white."
- "This has been such a useful tool. I wish I knew this stuff years ago."
- "This test gave me meaningful and relevant information with helpful suggestions."

You can take the *Money Chimp* test at:

www.moneychimp.net

In addition to the test, read books or do courses that help you explore your beliefs, skills and behaviours around money.

I highly recommend *The Energy of Money, The 4 Money Mindsets* and *Coach Yourself To Wealth*. You will find these books challenging because they will delve into your relationship with money starting from childhood. In my experience, you need to make time to understand your patterns and how you are wired up around money otherwise history will keep repeating itself.

The 4 Money Mindsets is an impeccable resource if you want to ensure you break out of a cycle of chronic debt.

I am sure your local library has both books and videos that are free to borrow at any time.

I also have a free *Facebook* group, *YouTube* videos; and podcasts on *Spotify* that unpack *The Money Chimp* with activities not in this book; and a community to get added support. Search *Multiply Your Money*.

The big take-away from this chapter should be: *Educate yourself about money.*

Your Turn

- Do you belong to a library? If so, go visit your local library and find the money section. See what books interest you. If not, join your local library and ...

- Borrow any book on debt reduction or saving money. Start there.

- Check the reference section at the back of this book for a list of books I highly recommend.

- *Google* search the Top 10 money saving websites.

- Have a look at the personal finance books on *Amazon*. There are lots! Here's a tip about *Amazon*. They sell both new and used copies. I recently found a great money book that was £26 new but only 40p used. Buy the used copies. I don't want you to go broke buying books on how to avoid going broke!

- Go to *Facebook* or *YouTube* or *Spotify* and search *Multiply Your Money* for some great free resources.

Money Skill #5 Taking Action

Let me emphasise that the ideas in this book *don't work*. What I mean is: they are totally worthless if you don't take any action. Good intentions and words *without actions* are meaningless.

The ideas don't work for you unless you work the ideas.

There is no point knowing something if you don't apply it. *To know and not to do is still not to know*. Re-read that last sentence several times!

This book may be interesting but totally useless if you don't take action.

You have to start somewhere. Think of it this way: you are not a victim to money. Money does not control you. Money is inanimate, lifeless. It's your beliefs, values and attitudes; your skills and competencies; and habits and behaviours that are the deciding factors. In some cases, you'll need to develop and persist with new habits.

I've given many examples throughout this book. In each case the ability to manage money improved dramatically by trying the ideas and giving them a fair test.

Most money managing books and courses say you have to spend less than you earn. That makes total sense, right?

They all suggest to pay yourself first or try and save at least 10% of your after-tax, take-home pay.

They all suggest you set money aside for emergencies.

Some suggest you get ahead by learning to live on less than 70% of your after-tax, take-home pay. We know that it's achievable and *most* people *can* get their finances under control within 90 days *and* even be debt free, but none of that will happen unless and until you take action.

The power is in the doing.

If you fail to take action then you need to ask yourself why. What's stopping you? And, like Jason, why exactly are you exempt from being responsible with your money?

You might have to collect receipts for at least three months before a clear picture emerges. I know most people will lose interest after a week but collect receipts anyway. Push through that inertia. You might have to start monitoring your spending more closely. Stick with it because results come very fast. You may have to trim back gently or drastically.

It might be embarrassing to ask for a receipt but that little piece of paper might be an important piece to your money puzzle if it highlights a dysfunctional money pattern.

Humans behave in highly predictable ways. We stick with familiar habits … even if those habits don't work!

Take smoking or drinking. Remember Luke? He drinks and smokes to feel accepted by his mates at the pub. Those mates buy each other drinks and share cigarettes but who really gets rich from smoking and drinking?

When Luke thought about it he secretly felt he was wasting his weekends at the pub watching football matches. He realised he was not really into rehashing football games either. He started to notice that he pretty much arrived at the bar on a Friday night and didn't go home until Sunday afternoon.

You may have to set some targets. It's not easy negotiating a new phone rate or gas bill or swapping energy providers. You can easily spend 20 minutes on hold.

It's not easy moving house but when you know you are paying £800 PCM more than you need to for the convenience of living ten minutes closer to work, it makes money sense.

You might need to trim your spending starting with eliminating items you don't really need to buy. You don't need new shoes each month. Or the latest version of *CoD, Halo* or *Grand Theft Auto*. Or a new smartphone on a 36-month payment plan. You don't need to spend £180 per week on alcohol.

You might need to take a second job just to pay off your credit card debt.

And you might need to get uncomfortable and read more books on managing money.

You might need to learn *impulse control* and *delayed gratification*. Most human problems come down to those two issues – the inability to resist impulses; and delay gratification.

The fact that you are sitting here right now not peeing your pants comes down to the ability to control urges and impulses. In the same way, you must learn to control the impulse to spend £400 a month on clothes to merely bolster your self-esteem and win approval.

I recently listened to Dr Craig Hassed and Stephen McKenzie's podcast on *mindfulness*. In one section, they explain how to cope with *urges*. Most urges really only last about ten minutes and then pass. If you have the urge to buy new shoes, go breathe instead! Focus on your in-breath and out-breath. If your mind wanders back to buying shoes, then just go back to focusing on your in and out-breath.

You might need to learn to say *No* to others – maybe family members or even yourself.

Delayed gratification means not spending now but instead saving money for a holiday, a car or a house deposit, later. Basically, you sacrifice the immediate gratification you get from spending right now, for something better in the future.

Every book I reviewed says save money first, and then invest. You cannot do the most basic investment strategies without some money behind you.

I think doing the money managing quiz is a great investment. I created *The Money Chimp* quiz to help you better understand your relationship with money and your current skills and habits. People worldwide say that the test is frighteningly accurate and incredibly helpful.

Reading books is an investment in your financial literacy.

So what if you find the book boring? Read another one. As I've said, every book says *none* of these ideas work unless you take action.

Your local bank has an excellent free service for anyone who needs to set up a household budget and special banking services such as a target account.

You can read books and do training courses on property investing. Doing a money workshop or spending a day with someone like Steve Bolton will give you much more than just good information.

Many training programmes include a community of like-minded people and a level of support you cannot get from a book.

You might join the *Multiply Your Money Facebook* group and start chatting with the people in that group. Sometimes the biggest insights come through informal conversations and by asking dumb questions.

Every book I read suggests seeking good advice. There are free and inexpensive advisory services; and high end advisors like financial advisors. You would be silly to doubt the need for financial advice.

And every book says take action.

Taking action is hard especially if you are trying to change long standing, years-old habits. It will feel like you're getting nowhere at first. Bank on it. But persist. Managing your money wisely is possibly the most important life-skill you will ever master.

Of course, you will benefit by re-reading this book several times. I am sure you will have missed a golden nugget buried inside this book.

Your Turn

- If you got this far you will definitely have some ideas to put into action. Write a list of obvious action steps and pick three – one hard and two easy - and get cracking.

- There are plenty of examples in this book of people who took simple actions and achieved great results. Remember the university students who cleared their credit card debt within three months? Which examples resonate with you most?

- Revisit the section on STOP, START and CONTINUE.

THE MONEY CHIMP

The Bonus Principle

There is a bonus principle hidden in this book. You may need to re-read this book to find it but I guarantee it will jump out at you.

If you want to be a champ, re-read this book anyway, because I know you will have missed a gold nugget.

That bonus principle is like a key that will open a door to success. It will turbo-charge your motivation to manage your money effectively. It will inspire you to become debt-free and even financially-free for life.

One reader said that the bonus principle that jumped out at him was *Get good advice*. It wasn't the one I deliberately buried but that's still pretty good!

So re-read each chapter and I guarantee you will experience a personally relevant light bulb moment that will change your life.

When that happens let me know.

Part 5

What To Do If You Are In Debt

THE MONEY CHIMP

Do You Have A Debt Problem?

Money worries live on a spectrum from *none, mild*, and *moderate* to *serious* and *extreme*. Which one sounds like you?

Any money worry can be frustrating or stressful even frightening but what's important is the belief you have in your own ability to sort them out.

If you know you have credit card debt but believe you could get your credit card debt under control easily, then yes, it's a money worry, but it's *mild*. However if you're worried sick and you can't sleep at night, or the bailiffs and repossessors are banging at the door, then it's serious, and you should seek help, today!

This book was designed to give information, practical help and encouragement. Sometimes distress over money is extreme. Sadly, a friend of mine committed suicide because his bills got out of control.

Don't panic. And don't isolate yourself.

No matter how hopeless things might seem and how despairing you feel, remember, help is always available.

To be clear, *The Money Chimp* is intended for people with mild to moderate money worries. In all cases you should feel you can take positive action, today, and start seeing results quickly. If you are like most people you will start to see positive results within the next 90 days if you start applying some of the recommendations in this book.

For if you complete the *The Money Chimp* quiz and recognise serious and extreme debt problems seek professional help from a qualified financial advisor, sooner. Even serious money worries can be turned around.

*The Money Chimp*quiz will give you a clear heads-up on your habits and skills and sometimes that's all that's needed to inspire you to take charge.

Take the test at *www.moneychimp.net*

For now, answer the questions below. Highlight the questions that apply to you:

- Do you usually run out of spending money before the end of the week?
- Do you often get bills you can't pay on time?
- Have you got more than two credit cards with constantly rising balances, fees and interest payments?
- Do you pay just the minimum amount off each card each month?
- Have you run up debts on store cards?
- Have you got loans?
- Do you miss loan repayments?
- Do you borrow to pay off your debts?

- Do you argue with your partner over money?
- Do you have trouble paying for the essentials - mortgage/rent, food, gas, electricity, phone etc?
- Do you regularly pay for basic living expenses such as groceries on your credit card because you have no cash?
- Do you receive 'disconnection' warning letters from suppliers or threatening 'demand' letters from debt collectors?
- Do you regularly borrow money from family or friends and hardly ever repay it?
- Do you resent people who have money?
- Do you think about winning the lottery as the solution to your money worries?

If you said YES to more than three of these questions you could have a debt problem. If so, you need to get advice about managing your money immediately. And you need to make reducing and clearing your debts a priority.

However there's a lot you can do right now that will steer you towards being debt-free.

Visit your local library

As mentioned most libraries have a vast selection of books and DVDs on money that cover the topics of *Earning, Spending, Saving, Investing* and *Giving* and the skills of *Monitoring, Focusing, Reducing, Developing* and *Taking Action*.

And better still everything is free or low cost.

I read over 143 books on managing personal finances and the full range of the five topics are fully covered in libraries!

Search the Internet

There is also an abundance of information online, but be careful. Make sure that it is current and relevant to *your* situation, your country and importantly, your tax laws.

Stay away from paid sites for now. Never supply your contact or credit card details to any online programmes, no matter how exciting or tempting. Some unscrupulous sites can start deducting regular payments without you even realising!

Some offer no-risk, money-back terms but in most cases getting your money back will be difficult. They have fine print. I once did a course that was total rubbish, that required me to prove that I had implemented the 60-day programme before I could be considered for a refund. *Be considered* ... amazing wording.

Seek help from professionals

If you are experiencing debt problems talk to a debt coach, a financial advisor or an accountant. Start with your bank and any of the government agencies that offer free or low-cost advice and support.

Rely on family or friends for support, not advice

Family members and friends are usually good for emotional support, but in my experience, very few are a reliable source of advice especially if they are financially struggling themselves. They may be well-intended but are usually misinformed and not up-to-date on current financial information.

Again, seek professional advice.

DIY courses

There are many self-help courses. Understand that if you do nothing else but learn how to closely monitor what you spend for the next 90 days you will start to improve your ability to manage your money.

Attend a scheduled workshop/course

Money Chimp offers online courses on managing personal finances but there are lots of free or low cost courses on offer close to where you live.

The *Citizens Advice Bureaux* in the UK can steer you towards reputable courses. Contact them at:

www.citizensadvice.org.uk

www.debt-help-pros.com/citizensadvice.php

Search *Citizens Advice Bureaux* in your country.

Tell the truth about what's happening

Far too often, I meet with people who are in trouble financially and they haven't shared that information with the people who matter most.

I recently chatted with a 30 year-old who was maxed out his credit card, was thousands of pounds in debt and hadn't told his girlfriend because ... he didn't want her to worry. This says a lot about personal honesty and integrity in the relationship.

As hard as it might be, you may need to start by being honest about what's happening.

Tell the truth, sooner

If you are debt, tell the truth to the people who matter most to you. Most people *can* handle the truth. What they can't handle is discovering you've known the truth for a long time and didn't tell them.

Telling the truth starts by gathering the facts so you can give an accurate picture.

Solving your money worries will take time, smart thinking and hard work. It may not be easy, but everyone who dug themselves out from under a mountain of debt applied the strategies in this book.

If all you can do right now is borrow a book from the library or visit a debt reduction or money managing website, then start there.

Managing your money is a lifelong skill. The good news is you can start to improve your financial situation within 90 days. You may not fix 100% but you will be better off by trying the basic suggestions recommended in this book.

This book gives you some of the tools to get you going.

If You Need To Be Debt-Free

Some people are a little in debt and some are deeply in debt. Irrespective of the size, if you have any debt problems, you need to take immediate action to control your debts over the next 90 days.

Here's what works consistently:

Gather up *every* money-related bill, statement and letter that you can find and collate them neatly in one folder.

Look for everything to do with your money such as receipts, bills and statements.

Sort them into categories

- Credit card statements
- Bank statements
- Charge card statements
- Loans statements
- Bills
- Debt repayment letters/demand notices

Get a complete list of every debt you owe, with the amount, plus the fees, charges and interest owed.

Top priority debts are:

- Mortgage/rent
- Loans such as student loans, housing loans
- Tax etc (HMRC, VAT etc)
- Council rates
- Utilities bills
- Licenses and registrations, TV, car etc.

These creditors *can and will* take *strong legal action* against you. Low priority debts are:

- Credit cards and charge cards
- Unsecured loans such as finance loans
- Overdrafts
- Store card purchases such as furniture
- Borrowings from family or friends

Warning: While these creditors are less pressing, you can still end up in court and be hit with the debts plus interest, *and the legal costs.* Yours *and* theirs. *So be warned.*

Only seek help from qualified advisors

Start with the *Citizens Advice Bureaux*. Ultimately, the key is to create a reduction plan that suits your circumstances. Once you have that plan contact everyone you owe money to and keep them informed. And then stick to the plan. Do not ignore your creditors.

Avoid High Street short-term, money lenders. The offer a quick fix loaded up with super high interest charges. These loans are dangerous because they typically start a new cycle of debt that worsens your situation. Buries you deeper.

If you are in financial trouble

Your number one goal is to get out of debt. Out of financial trouble! Once debt-free, you can start fresh with the principle of spending less than what you earn.

Credit and store card debts are crushing. Credit cards make it very easy to have what you want instantly! But this is a serious mistake especially if you cannot manage your money.

Grow up. The real problem is a lack of self-discipline.

As I've said, the fastest escape route from financial woes is to save 10% of your after-tax, take-home pay - no matter what; reduce your debts with 20% of your income; and learn to live on 70% of your take-home pay.

If you are in serious financial trouble, start with the *Citizens Advice Bureaux* in your country.

In most cases, they can *quickly* assess your needs, devise a debt-reduction plan, point you in the right direction, get you started, and support you in becoming debt-free.

Never be tempted to do anything illegal!

Countless people make life worse by trying to solve financial difficulties by doing something illegal i.e., scams, drug dealing. Even starting a cash-only business like ironing or housecleaning will get you into trouble if you don't declare your earnings.

A friend of mine is a UK money-laundering expert. You suddenly pay cash for something and quicker than you would believe you will end up on the wrong side of the law if you can't explain where the money came from. The fines are hefty, the jail terms lengthy.

Use your loaf, my grandmother used to said.

Don't do anything stupid or desperate

Recently there was a $303 million lottery jackpot in America. I read about a young man - deeply in debt - who took his life savings *and* borrowed thousands to buy hundreds of lottery tickets. *None of them won.*

I recently heard of a guy who transferred all his life savings to a *lawyer* in Nigeria who said a relative had died and left him $14 million in cash and all he needed to do was to transfer $15,000 to process the stamp duty. Of course, this was a blatant scam. (Just consider this: even if it were true just imagine how you might ship *$14 million in cash* back to your country, and getting that through customs. Some people just do not think it through. Or what bank would you put it in that doesn't have a tax treaty with your country? If you even accept, technically, you might already have committed a felon in several jurisdictions.)

Sadly, there are ruthless people who prey on the vulnerable. If you are in debt you are not thinking clearly and highly susceptible to scams. I know this for a fact.

Don't do anything expensive

There are people who claim they can help you for a fee. But don't get conned into paying fees for advice that is general and freely available.

Start with free government agencies.

Don't do anything that promises a big return for no effort

I recently chatted with a plumber that bought a course in professional speaking on the promise that he would have a fast entry, side-door entry into professional speaking. He was earning £26,000 pa, and in debt and the course was £13,000 - half his income! The deal was £1,000PCM for 13 months.

In his mind, he imagined *quickly* and *easily* being a highly sought after motivational speaker earning a six figure income.

This guy was, dare I say, caught up in the fantasy. The reality of that industry is like any other profession - grit and graft. I asked if I could fast track being a plumber and he said it isn't possible. I said professional speaking is just the same.

Undeterred, he signed up and after three months discovered that it was a LOT harder than he expected and demanding of time and money. Plus they wanted to upsell him into a buying video production show reels.

He managed to get out of that contract, but £3,600 poorer. In my experience, if its quick and easy it probably won't be good.

Start where you are right now

Remember Jake? He started cleaning the windows and front yards of homes in his street. Most of his clients lived within half a mile of his home and pretty soon he was earning $15 per hour, six hours a day, five days a week. Potentially, that's $450 a week!

Did he want to be a cleaner? No. He is saving up to buy camera equipment because he wants to be a portrait photographer. But for now, he is a cleaner. And with his determination he will get there.

Money equals taxes ... somewhere

I have a *PayPal* account, originally for *eBay* sales, and now my USD$ information product sales. I also use *Square* for credit card sales worldwide. That money lives in cyberbanks, somewhere.

I know people that leave it in cyberbanks and use, say their *PayPal* account, to buy clothing or furniture. Small amounts.

At some point, if the totals are significant, it makes sense to repatriate the money. Whatever you do don't try and evade paying tax.

I have a friend that is based in the UK but has an Australian bank account. He moved the money from *PayPal* to Australia but was then queried by the bank who liaised with the *Australian Tax Office (ATO)* because they suspected money laundering. The *ATO* has a tax treaty with the UK, so then *HMRC* got involved. And ... and ... and ...

Get the idea?

I download monies to my UK bank account, declare it and pay tax. No problems.

The moral is please: don't try and evade paying taxes. Mitigate your tax bill but don't do anything that feels like tax evasion.

Your Turn

- When people are under pressure they make dumb choices. Period. Can you recall a time when this accurately described your behaviour? How did that work out for you?
- Make a list of any dumb ideas you are considering especially any that involve illegality or tax avoidance. Then take them off your to-do list.

Will You Learn To Manage You Money And *Stay Out Of Debt?*

Let me repeat the good news. You can learn to manage your money and be debt-free within 90 days ... but will you *stay* out of debt?

Wealth coach, Karen Sutton-Johal understands chronic debt better than most. She grew up in a family that experienced a continuous cycle of crippling debt. But she learned how to exit that cycle - *and stay out of debt* - and now teaches others how to do the same.

She has an interesting observation: "I specialise in helping people get debt-free by applying some practical tools and skills.

"But I noticed that my clients often *went straight back to being in debt again.* I realised that what needs to change is your mind-set. You really do have to think differently about money if you are in debt. I honestly believe it's because you have a *debt mind-set.*"

Karen has identified four money mind-sets:

- Debt
- Break-even
- Comfortable and
- Rich (financially free)

Having helped thousands of clients get out of debt and stay out of debt, she says the key to staying debt-free is shifting your mind-set.

"I can get you out of debt but unless you change your mind-set and relationship with money you will most likely be back in debt sooner or later, and usually sooner. But in most cases, you will make the problem worse."

Changing your mind-set starts with deciding to manage your money better. You can make the life changing decision to be debt-free and financially free. Start thinking and acting differently in your attitudes to money.

You might need help from a wealth coach or a financial advisor. Investing in your financial education is wort while.

Start the process by reading books.

A Final Word On Credit Cards

Do you have a credit card? Do you always pay off the outstanding balance by the end of the month? If so, well done! You are an exception to the rule!

I have encouraged you to reduce or eliminate credit card debt because it is the number one problem for young adults.

Banks and credit card companies profit from interest fees and charges from people who cannot pay off the outstanding monthly balance.

Debt charities like *StepChange*, exist to offer free advice and solutions for people struggling with debt problems. *StepChange* estimate that the majority of their clients suffer from credit card debt and the average household debt exceeds £9,000.

StepChange reported that over 14 million people in 2015 experienced *income shock* through GFC-related circumstances. Over four million relied on credit to cover basic necessities. And people who rely on their credit card to cope are 20 times more likely to enter a long-term crippling debt cycle.

According to the *Financial Conduct Authority*, credit card debt in 2015 was around £61 billion with a disturbing number of consumers in arrears; or defaulting. In 2019, that figure rose to £72.5 billion.

They suggest that too many credit card users only manage to

make minimum monthly repayments to cover interest. If this sounds like you then you can easily find yourself paying off a credit card balance for years.

Understand, it is not the job of a credit card company to manage your money. That is your job. They are in the business of earning interest from lending money.

Credit card debt is insidious and if you have an outstanding balance that isn't reducing you should make this a focus of action.

I have given several inspiring examples of young people who reduced or totally eliminated their credit card debts. In every case, it took hard work and focused effort. But they did it.

Here's a sample of websites you might explore if you have debt problems. These resources will help you with information and support.

www.moneyadviceservice.org.uk

www.adviceuk.org.uk

www.stepchange.org

www.nationaldebtline.org

www.businessdebtline.org

www.capuk.org

www.citizensadvice.org.uk

www.debtadvicefoundation.org

Oh yes ... Black Friday, Cyber Monday, Christmas, Boxing Day, January Sales ...

Black Friday is the name given to the retail shopping day in November after Thanksgiving in the US. It was originally called *Black Friday* because the sheer volume of shoppers created queuing, traffic accidents and sometimes even violence but it can also suggest it's the day when retailers financially go from being in the *red* to being in the *black*.

Black Friday has historically been the busiest shopping day, now week, of the year in the United States since 2005, averaging about $50 billion plus and growing. And now, it is a worldwide phenomena.

In the UK, there is now a one week lead up to *Black Friday* as well. It's also the week that most Brits get paid before Christmas.

Cyber Monday, is the online version.

In any case, the goal is to part you from your money. I understand why retailers do it. But from my perspective this is the start of one of the most stressful times of the year.

I was chatting with a client who has two teenagers. Both want a new laptop and a smartphone. Conservatively, that's about £3,000 per child. He already knows they will be disappointed if they receive anything less, or the wrong brand, and he already feels anxious and guilty that they will be.

This is not Christmas. Christmas is about joy not about fear.

Last year, a client spend £7,500 on Christmas presents. Another spent £17,000 on outfits because she couldn't be seen wearing the same outfit at the staff and business functions she attended. Both were still paying off Christmas in June six months later. Plus the fees and charges.

In addition, people are now conflicted about buying gifts for Christmas Day, knowing that on Boxing Day the sales start. In Australia, it used to be the *January Sales* but time is money and its all been dialled back to December 26.

Juxtaposed against *Crisis At Christmas*, and the *Red Cross* and *Salvation Army Christmas Appeal* for the destitute and homeless this is rampant commercialism at its very worst. I usually ask people to donate £5 to their favourite charity such as *WaterAid, The Hunger Project, Unicef, Clear Sky Childrens Charity* or some other reputable charity like *The Big Issue, Crisis, The Salvation Army* or *Red Cross*.

How I do Christmas

I love Christmas. For years now I have saved £100 per month and in December I have £1,200 to spend on catering and small gifts. As a family we have focused gift giving on grandchildren but we keep it low key. Birthdays are now the time for special gifts.

I have said its good to give as long as it doesn't hurt the giver.

Can I suggest that you think about creating a Christmas Savings account so that you know exactly know how much you have to spend and the money is there.

For me, Christmas is a special time in the Christian calendar that becomes more important each year from a faith perspective.

What is Christmas like for you? If Christmas could be a joy, what would that look like?

Let Me Know How You Are Going

I am pleased to say the ideas in *The Money Chimp* work! *The Money Chimp* was a bestseller in 2016 and has been in and out of the Top 20 UK money books since.

But only you can prove that for yourself. I love hearing success stories and getting feedback. Judging by the emails I receive worldwide, *The Money Chimp* is changing lives for the better.

I encourage you to go to *Facebook* and join the *Multiply Your Money* group. There is a lot of great stuff inside that group like videos, links, downloadable handouts; and a supportive community.

I encourage you to share your journey with the group.

Also search *Multiply Your Money* on *YouTube;* and the podcast on *Spotify*.

If you go to www.andrewpriestley.com and navigate to the *Resources* page you can access the companion book *How Money Flows Through Your Business*. This is a powerful resource if you own a business because it explains business money in plain English and includes a 90 minute video workshop and resources.

THE MONEY CHIMP

References

- Aaron, Raymond. (2008). *Double Your Income By Doing What You Love*, Wiley.
- Bachrach, Bill. (2000). *Values Based Financial Planning*, A m High Publishing.
- Bolton, Steve. (2012). *Successful Property Investing: How to Earn £50,000 to £150,000 in Two to Five Years*, A Platinum Partners Press Book.
- Clason, George, S. (1926). *The Richest Man In Babylon*, Hawthorn/Dutton.
- Conwell, Russell. (1915). *Acres of Diamonds*.
- Coonradt, Charles et al. (1996). *The Four Laws of Debt Free Prosperity, Chequemate International*.
- Eisenberg, Lee. (2006). *The Number*, Free Press.
- Grant, Patrick. (2015). *Planning For Retirement,* Straightforward Guides.
- Kelley, Sarano. (2001). *The Game*. Jodere Group.
- Kiyosaki, Robert. (1997). *Rich Dad, Poor Dad*. TechPress, Inc.
- Lewis, Martin. (2005).*The Money Diet*. Vermilion.
- Lewis, Martin. (2006). *Thrifty Ways For Modern Days*. Vermilion
- Lewis, Martin. (2008). *The Three Most Important Lessons You've Never Been Taught*. Vermilion
- Nemeth, Maria. (1997). *The Energy of Money,* Ballatine Wellspring.

- Mathew, Diana. (1996). *The Money Tree,* National Direct Marketing.
- McKinnon, Shirley. (2001). *Coach Yourself To Wealth*, Crown Content.
- Millar, Caroline Adams. (2009). *Creating Your Best Life,* Sterling.
- Nutting, John. (2015). *Growing Awareness.* Nutting.
- Prochanska, James, O. et al. (1994). *Changing For Good: A Revolutionary Six-Stage Program For Overcoming Bad Habits And Moving Your Life Positively Forward.* Collins Living.
- Richards, Carl. (2015). *The One Page Financial Plan: A Simple Way To Be Smart About Your Money.* Psychologies, October 2015.
- Schafer, Bodo. (1999). *The Road To Financial Freedom*, Griffin Press.
- Stanton, Dr. Harry E. (1979). *The Plus Factor,* Optima Books.
- Stanton, Dr. Harry E. (1997). *Let the Trade Winds Flow.*
- Ward, Nigel. (2013). *Using Less Stuff.* Writing Matters Publishing.
- Warner, Stuart. (2010). *Secrets Finance Basics,* Harper Collins.
- Wilson, Ann. (2014). *The Wealth Chef.* Hay House.
- Wusche, Vicki. (2010). *How to Invest in Property.* SRA Books.
- Wusche, Vicki. (2012) . *Property for the Next Generation: Preparing Your Family for a Wealthy Future.* SRA Books

About Andrew Priestley

Andrew Priestley is an award winning, business coach who specialises in the psychology of achievement. He coaches clients worldwide.

He wrote *The Money Chimp* because too many of his professional clients have great incomes but are broke. They do not understand basic personal finances let alone business finance.

The Money Chimp helps professionals spend less, save more and get out of credit card debt faster. In most cases readers will experience a significant change in their finances within 90 days.

After an extensive review of money managing literature, he wrote *The Money Chimp* and created the *The Money Chimp* quiz to help people identify their money managing strengths and weaknesses; and acquire skills in managing money.

He has added *YouTube* videos and a popular podcast on *Spotify* called *Multiply Your Money*.

Andrew says: "Young professionals aged 18-25 are typically the most susceptible to entering a cycle of chronic debt. I really hope the habits and skills featured in *The Money Chimp* set you on the road to financial freedom."

THE MONEY CHIMP

Contacts And Links

Business coaching

www.andrewpriestley.com

linkedin.com/in/andrewpriestley

https://andrewpriestley.com/resources/downloads/

The Money Chimp Test

www.moneychimp.net

THE MONEY CHIMP

Printed in Great Britain
by Amazon